Contents

Introduction

Even before our earliest ancestors were learning to forge tools, cultivate food, domesticate animals, and create vessels from clay, they were making baskets. Prehistoric food gatherers, out on foraging expeditions in the forests and jungles and in need of containers to transport the fruits of their labor, folded a piece of bark or interwove leaves and grasses to construct the first crude and temporary baskets. When the immediate need no longer existed, the basket was discarded. The materials themselves were so perishable that few of these early baskets remain. Instead, we must be satisfied with the information provided by anthropologists and with the evidence of basketmaking traditions that have survived, almost unchanged, over the ages.

At some point, a remarkable transition was made from the rough and temporary baskets of prehistory to the specialized vessels of today, constructed in advance of need and over a long period of time for permanence and durability. Baskets of the permanent variety were used by these societies much as we use containers of plastic and metal today: to carry food and personal items, to store, cook, trap, and strain. In addition, they were used in child care and for adornment and protection. Ultimately, the most sophisticated basketmakers used baskets as a form of artistic or religious expression.

Basketry is still a significant craft in some of the less mechanized regions of the world: the baskets pouring into our markets from Africa and the Orient attest to the viability of the craft. In addition, we are in the midst of a reappraisal of our own rich traditions—as in our current and long overdue interest in the baskets of the American Indians. We are also experiencing a growing concern with the environment and its proper utilization. The basketmaker becomes deeply involved with the rhythms of nature by participating in the raising, conservative gathering, and careful preparation of materials for the making of baskets. But we can be forward-looking as well, for the products of modern society are also suitable for making baskets. Rope, yarn, metallics, and plastics can be worked side-by-side with reeds, raffia, vines, and splints.

It is our hope in this book to provide an introductory guide to creative basketry. No prior knowledge of basketmaking is necessary. The minimal equipment needed will be described, and the techniques for constructing and decorating coiled and woven baskets will be discussed and illustrated. As a result, the novice will learn how to begin, stitch, shape, and finish several kinds of baskets. Moreover, the projects have been designed to include a variety of techniques, materials, and shapes, giving the new basketmaker a wide range to build upon. Along with complete instructions, a list of mail-order suppliers is provided to increase one's access to all the materials mentioned. Photographs of outstanding traditional and contemporary baskets and basket forms have been included for illustration and inspiration. It is hoped that the reader will use these examples, suggestions, and techniques as a foundation for experimenting with materials and forms in order to create truly individual baskets.

Inexpensive samples taken from the authors' collections show a wide variety of coiled and woven basketry techniques, functions, and designs.

Equipment and Materials

EQUIPMENT

One of the beauties of basketry is that the small number of tools needed for the making of baskets requires no great expenditure either of energy or of money on the part of the craftsperson.

Basic needs include a good work space, a source of water, and a place for soaking materials. If the worktable is far from a sink or bathtub, a small pan may be used to keep soaking materials close at hand. A towel for absorbing excess moisture and drying hands, a comfortable chair or stool, and a good source of light are also helpful.

A variety of tools may be used to shape and cut materials: a pair of scissors or a sharp knife is a necessity (we prefer an X-Acto knife), reed cutters may be purchased from some basketry suppliers if desired, and the round-nosed pliers sometimes used to squeeze reed before bending (to prevent it from cracking) are found at hardware stores.

A small, easily held awl, also found at hardware or sewing supplies stores, is used to make spaces for new materials, to ease the passage of the needle in coiled work, and to form holes in shells.

As for the needle, a no. 18 tapestry needle with a blunt end is the most versatile. The blunt end will be kinder than a sharp one on the materials and fingers, and the eye will accommodate most thicknesses of yarn or raffia. Keep six to twelve needles on hand.

Crochet hooks or screwdrivers help lift materials out of the way and allow access to those hard-to-get-at spaces. Clothespins hold materials in place, and sewing thread temporarily binds splices until they are secured by stitching or weaving. A tape measure is useful for keeping track of size; graph paper for working out designs; paper and pen or pencil for taking notes and keeping records. For those who gather materials, a camera will help in recording gathering sites.

The most basic and most important tools of all are the hands. Keeping them and other tools clean will keep materials clean and, thus, affect the overall appearance of your work. Hands can become dry as moisture is absorbed by the materials during basketmaking, so hand cream could be kept near the work area.

MATERIALS

Just as the earliest peoples created baskets spontaneously to fulfill the needs of the moment, so also did they choose from the green materials at hand to form those temporary baskets. In the jungles and tropics, palm and other leaves were available; in the forest, there were ferns and tree barks, young shoots, and roots of trees; marshes and meadows yielded a variety of tall grasses and leaves.

As baskets became more permanent (that is, fashioned in advance and with a particular purpose in mind) specific fibers were sought out for their durability and flexibility, for their attractive texture or color, as well

Facing page: A variety of gathered, commercial, and synthetic basketry materials

as for their availability. In order to avoid the shrinkage and cracking that baskets woven with fresh materials are subject to, regional and tribal traditions evolved for the gathering, curing, and preparation of materials, with set schedules and procedures handed down from generation to generation.

In the modern world, some basketmakers are able to move easily from one region to another to pick a variety of materials at appropriate times of the year. Many materials that cannot be gathered can be bought in standard sizes and/or quantities from importers and mail-order suppliers. Regardless of the source, it is important for the craftsperson to know about the proper handling of all materials.

When gathering basketry materials, the primary rule remains one of conservation: harvest with care, take only what is needed without depleting any plant in one spot, and leave the roots intact whenever possible.

The chart at the end of this section gives basic information about the gathering, curing, and use of those natural materials most readily available; however, a chart cannot offer extensive detailed instructions and is included here more as a suggestion than as a major resource. The Natural Basketry Bibliography on page 64 lists several books that focus on this subject area.

Commercially prepared materials are usually fully processed prior to distribution, although woody materials such as the rattan palm products —round reed, flat reed, and cane—must be made flexible by soaking before actual work on the basket begins. If materials are purchased directly from those who did the actual gathering, processing may be incomplete. At the time of purchase, ask for specific information about the materials—identification, storage problems, traditional use, and additional preparation required.

Below: Jacqueline Davidson used plastic coated wire and plastic tubing for her "Canal Street Basket # 1." The feet are electrical components and the basket is 7½" x 3". *Below right:* Gary Trentham used all natural linen in this 5½" x 7½" coiled basket. The surface texture was created by twisting knots until they curled up on themselves (called "overtwisting"). Photo by John P. Creel III.

The natural materials already mentioned, whether gathered by the basketmaker or commercially processed, can be supplemented by contemporary materials that previously had other primary functions—for example, yarns from weavers' studios, cordage and ropes and wires from hardware stores and workshops, and plastics from industry. With continued experimentation, new materials and uses will emerge. The basketmaker can turn a newly sensitized eye to clotheslines, bamboo skewers, packing cords, and even newspapers.

With such a wealth of materials to choose from, it would make matters easy if one could simply consult a list to see how each material is best used. However, such a list would be more limiting and misleading than helpful. Instead, the sections on Coiling and Weaving Techniques include information on materials, with the emphasis given to the relationship between basket function, techniques, design, and material choice. Novice basketmakers will then have a base of information upon which to build as they continue with the projects.

Gathered Materials

Materials	Part Used	When Gathered	Curing Process	Common/Traditional Use
cattails (rush)	leaves	summer—fall	dry in loose bundles, turn frequently	twined or plaited baskets, mats
cedarbark	strips of inner bark	from felled trees	strip, scrape	twined or plaited mats, clothing
cornhusks	husks only	harvest	dry, store flat	twined or coiled bags, decorative material
ferns	stems	end of growing season	dry, remove leaves	twining weft, coiling foundation
vines and runners: honeysuckle, virginia creeper, wisteria, others	long runner	anytime	wind into coils, dry, store; can be boiled and scraped	wickerwork or twining
bulb plants: iris, tulip, day lily, etc.	leaves only	only when dry to protect bulb	dry completely, bundle for storage	coiling foundation and binder, twining weft
palm	fronds	anytime	dry, store; can be used green	plaiting, some twining
pine	needles	spring or summer—green; fall—brown	dry, bundle for storage	coiling—bundle foundation
grasses	blades	anytime	dry, store in bundles	coiling—bundle foundation
splint	log itself	from felled trees	complex—see bibliography	plaiting, splintwork

Natural Dyeing

It is possible that a basketmaker may spend many years creating baskets without ever needing to dye materials—such is the wealth of color in the natural materials themselves and in those dyed materials that may be purchased from suppliers. But for those who have planned a project with a specific color in mind and have been unable to find it and for those who wish to enjoy another adventure related to the textile arts, dyeing basketry materials with natural dyes is suggested.

With simple instructions available, it is possible initially to experiment with dyeing without making a costly commitment. There is such a variety of dyestuffs to consider that one may gather in the woods, the back yard, the market, or the mail-order catalogue with equal success. For example, a range of yellows and oranges can be produced with wild goldenrod, marigold blossoms, or tumeric raided from the kitchen spice shelf. Cochineal, an aphid that lives on cactus and which may be purchased in a pulverized state from supply houses, provides a brilliant red dye. Lovely shades of olive and lime come from green carrot tops, which are often discarded by those produce stands that still sell fresh, unbagged carrots.

From antiquity, the source of the best blue dye has been the indigo plant; its natural powder gives a beautiful shade of turquoise and its extract yields a pure blue. Mixing blue and red dyes produces violet, a color that can also be obtained from the bark of the logwood tree. One of the richest and most colorfast browns comes from the hulls of the black walnut—the dye is so strong that it will stain your fingers if you don't wear rubber gloves. Old coffee grounds and tea bags provide a nice range of beiges, and a dye extract of strong, cold tea may "antique" a basket, giving it new richness and sending the creator back to the dyepot for more of the magic of emerging color.

Although natural dye color can rarely be duplicated in subsequent dyebaths, this seeming inconsistency is compensated for by the unique, rich tones that can be achieved. Dyeing allows the craftsperson control over yet another factor in the creative process.

The books and publications listed in the Natural Dyeing Bibliography on page 64 give information on preparing natural dyes.

Left: Twined pouch (in progress), 20″ x 7″, was started at the top (see page 34). Linen warp and a weft of naturally dyed raffia split into fine strands were used. Goldenrod, indigo, cochineal, and onion skins provided the color, and variations on plain twining produced the design effects. The diamond shapes were accomplished with false embroidery. By Rachel Seidel Gilman. *Below:* In Virginia Davis' coiled basket form, 18″ x 3′, irregularly placed openwork stitches of cochineal-dyed yarn reveal a foundation of white cotton piping.

Construction Techniques: Coiled Basketry

When a person unfamiliar with crafts thinks of basketry, it is usually of baskets made in one or another variety of weaving. However, our markets are equally full of baskets made in a technique called coiling, which cannot truly be described as weaving; rather, it is a stitching technique in which the continuous coils of a foundation or substructure are interconnected by a binding element in a variety of stitches. In this technique, the binder can be poked through holes made in the foundation itself, can be passed on a needle through a non-rigid foundation, or can bind two foundation coils together by stitching around them.

This chapter is intended to be a guide to the making of coiled baskets: it shows several methods for beginning these baskets, a large variety of stitches that can be used in this technique, and various methods of splicing materials. In addition, there is a discussion of the design elements involved, including the formation of handles and lids.

GLOSSARY

Coiling—a type of basketwork in which a foundation, or core of material, is arranged in a spiral and held together by means of stitching with a binding material.

Foundation—the core material that is held in place by stitching with a second, less rigid material; *working foundation* or *new foundation* refers specifically to foundation material as yet uncovered by stitching; *foundation bundle* refers specifically to a foundation comprising separate elements held together in a group and, thus, utilized as a single unit.

Binder—a flexible material used to sew foundation coils together; the binder may be worked on a needle, or, if more rigid, may be placed through spaces created with a pointed instrument; binder is always finer and more flexible than foundation material.

Stitch—a movement in which the binder actually *secures* the working (new) foundation to the previous coil; the stitching process may completely or partially cover the foundation material with binder.

Wrap—a movement, as opposed to the *stitch,* defined above, in which the binder covers (wraps) *only* the working foundation and does not secure or involve the previous coil.

Overhand Knot—the most basic knot, in which one end of a strand (or group of strands) is drawn through a loop and the loop is then tightened (see diagram).

Ply—an element or strand of yarn or rope; *single-ply* indicates a yarn composed of one strand, *two-ply* indicates a yarn composed of two strands twisted together, and so on.

Splice—to join materials at their end points; for yarns, cords, and ropes,

Overhand knot

this involves unplying, tapering, and retwisting; for reeds and other rigid materials, this involves tapering and securing.

Start—the initial unit around which foundation material will coil; for coiled baskets this is usually at the center of the base (bottom). The start chosen for each basket is determined by the intended function of the work and the materials used.

Starting Position—used as a means of orienting worker to work; the needle is held in the stitching hand and above the work, which is held in the opposite hand; the point where stitching and wrapping occurs is usually at the top of the work; the work is usually turned clockwise as binder progresses counterclockwise around the coil.

Working Away from You—refers only to the relationship of the binder to the working foundation and means binder passes *in front of* the working foundation and then over the top *away* from the basketmaker (see diagram).

Working Toward You—as above, this refers only to the relationship of the binder to the working foundation—the binder passes *behind* the working foundation and then over the top *toward* the basketmaker (see diagram).

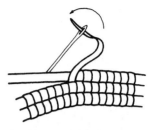

Working away from you

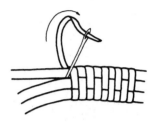

Working toward you

Material Selection

When reading through the following sections, which discuss specific coiling techniques (starts, stitches, finishes, etc.), try to keep in mind how these discussions and descriptions relate to the selection of materials. Occasionally you may construct a basket with little thought to the materials—perhaps simply utilizing whatever is handy or leftover from other projects. Most often, however, the need for or intended use of the basket is defined first, and that factor affects all other decisions that follow.

A great variety of materials may be used for making coiled baskets. The *foundation* should be firm enough to hold the shape of the basket but flexible enough to form the spiral or coil. It can comprise a single long length of material, shorter lengths that can be spliced to form the long, continuous spiral, or bunches of material grouped together to form a foundation bundle. Reeds, cords, vines, willow, leaves, bunches of grass, yarn, rope, and so on are possible choices from among the vast group of suitable materials. The *binder* in a coiled basket is always finer and more flexible than the foundation and should be suited to the stitch chosen and the function of the basket. Within these limitations, almost anything can be used for binder, including roots, raffia, yarn, leaves, and linen thread.

Although more a matter of logic than formula, some specific information on material selection is included here, with the hope that it will stimulate the reader to further thought as reading and work continue.

As an example for discussion, baskets that are strictly utilitarian—especially those used for carrying heavy items—require materials with certain characteristics. These materials must take stress well, not lose

Stitching on outside of basket, on side closest to basketmaker

Stitching on inside of basket, on side opposite (farthest away from) basket-maker

their shape with extensive use, and not fall apart when they come into occasional contact with water (which is inevitable with utility baskets). For foundations, woody materials, such as round reed and willow, automatically come to mind, although firm cords may be equally serviceable if they are aesthetically suited to the specific basket. Because the stitches in such baskets must be closely spaced for stability, the flexibility of the binder and the stitch used must be carefully considered (e. g., linen or several strands of raffia for a binder and the Figure-Eight stitch would be appropriate).

The same careful planning and selection procedures used with utilitarian baskets can benefit the basketweaver when planning other work. We wish to emphasize the variety of materials, traditional and unusual, available to the basketmaker. When choosing materials for a project, consider making several samples, finally selecting those materials that are both aesthetically pleasing and functional—that is, appropriate to the intended use of the basket.

Note: It is important to realize that using rigid material (such as round reed) for the foundation does *not* guarantee a sturdy basket. A basket constructed solely of rug yarn and utilizing the techniques of the Central Knot start and the Figure-Eight stitch could easily be more stable than a basket of similar shape using round reed and raffia, particularly if the latter was stitched carelessly—that is, with slack tension and too many wraps between stitches.

Orientation

The orientation used on all the following diagrams is that of one of the authors (right-handed); the materials and start are held in the left hand and the needle with binder in the right. If the reader finds this orientation awkward, then transpose and work in the opposite direction. It should be noted that not all left-handed students find it necessary to do so, but to those who must make the adjustment (which, incidentally, includes the other author), we extend an apology in advance.

When you are stitching, the surface that is *facing* you, that is, either the inside or the outside, will be the one that shows the stitches to their best advantage. (Usually the side that will be most visible is chosen for the best side.) Most of our examples are constructed so that the stitching looks best on the *outside* of the basket; thus, the *outside* of the basket faces the basketmaker and the stitching is done on the side of the basket *closest to* the basketmaker (see top photo). When making a basket in which the interior will be viewed most, for example, a large, shallow bowl, the reverse is done. Then, the *inside* of the basket faces the basketmaker and the stitching is placed on the side of the basket *opposite* (farthest away from) the basketmaker (see bottom photo).

Starts

The choice of start is usually determined by the function of the basket, the shape desired (round or oval), and the adaptability of the material to certain techniques (e. g., rigid material is not suitable for foundation when using the Central Knot start). Sometimes the start is determined by the materials at hand. For example, if a basket is to be constructed from leftover yarn, then the Central Knot is the most obvious choice—or, another possibility for the basket would be to choose a different material for the start and to introduce the yarn as a foundation bundle after the start is completed. It should be noted that once the start is achieved, it is a simple process to change to a different foundation material (see diagram e, Central Knot start, page 19, as an example). The limitations of each start will be discussed in the instructions that follow.

Keep in mind, for all starts, that the direction the binder travels, that is *toward* or *away from* the basketmaker, is specified for each stitch to allow for proper stitching procedure. The Lazy Squaw stitch, for example, dictates that the binder move *toward* the weaver, while the Figure-Eight stitch calls for the binder to move *away*. (See section on Stitches, pages 20–21.)

CIRCULAR START FOR A ROUND BASKET

The Circular start is a simple adaptation of the classic Navajo start used in continuous-coil baskets. It is ideal for the novice, as it uses readily available material, is easily understood and executed, and proceeds quickly. The start has the disadvantage of a small hole at its center and so it would not be suitable for all baskets.

The plant fibers of willow and grasses that the Navajos used are now rarely chosen. Instead, a firm rope, jute cord, or heavy yarn is often used for the foundation and a more flexible, lightweight yarn or cord is used for the binder. With the same type of foundation, a natural material such as day-lily leaves or raffia may be easily substituted as binder; the resulting basket would be similar in appearance to the original Navajo.

To begin, cut a yard-long piece of binder, and thread the needle with the binding material. Hold the tail end of the binder along the foundation and one inch from the foundation's end (see diagram a), and wrap away from you around both the tail and the foundation for a length long enough to form a small circle—approximately one inch. Make sure the foundation is completely covered. Then taper the unwrapped foundation end by untwisting the plies to the point where you started wrapping and cutting off all but one ply (see diagram b). Form a circle with the wrapped area (see diagram c), hold the single ply against the foundation, and wrap both together for one inch (see diagram d). Fold this last inch back against the original circle and hold securely so that the first stitch may be taken (see diagram e). For the first row of stitches, insert the needle into the center of the circle.

The Circular start is now complete, and the basketmaker must choose which stitches are to be used for the rest of the basket.

Circular Start for a Round Basket

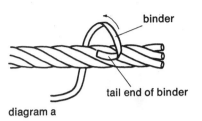

diagram a

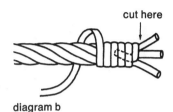

diagram b

diagram c

diagram d

diagram e

TWO SQUARE STARTS FOR A ROUND BASKET WITH A BUNDLE FOUNDATION

These two Square starts are found most typically in baskets of the Pima and Papago Indian tribes of the southwestern United States. Although these Indians use strips of the yucca plant, we may substitute any flexible material, such as yarn, raffia, or grasses. In addition, the size of the central formation may be varied by beginning with a different number of strips of foundation material.

For the first Square start, begin with six strands of foundation material that are eighteen inches long and of even width. Lay a vertical group of three strands across a horizontal group of three strands so they cross at the center (see diagram a). Fold the left-hand half of the horizontal strands over the vertical strands and diagonally up to the upper right corner (see diagram b). Then, *always folding over;* fold the top half of the vertical strands to the lower right corner (diagram c), the right-hand half of the horizontal strands to the lower left corner (diagram d), and the bottom half of the verticals to the upper left corner (diagram e), each in its turn. Insert the last group (the bottom half of the verticals) through the loop formed by the first fold (see diagram f), and pull the resulting four groups of strands tight to secure the start (see diagrams g and h); it may be necessary to tighten each strand individually. To make the start two-faced (if both inside and outside are to look the same), turn the entire unit over and repeat the process. *Note:* The appearance of this start may vary considerably depending on the firmness and size of the materials used.

For the second Square start, begin with eight strips of foundation material. Lay four strips on a table parallel to one another. Perpendicular

First Square Start

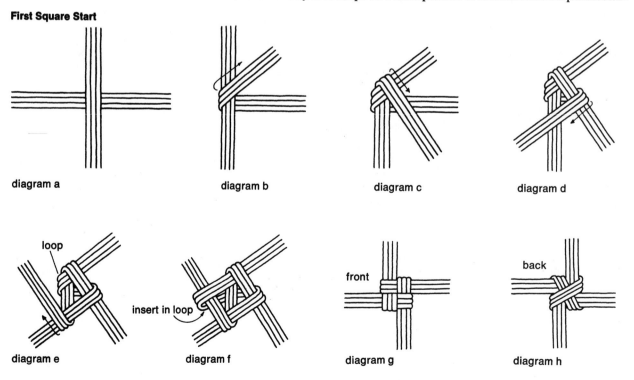

diagram a   diagram b   diagram c   diagram d

diagram e   diagram f   diagram g   diagram h

to these, weave the fifth strip over one, under one, over one, under one. The sixth strip will weave under one, over one, under one, over one. Continue for seventh and eighth strips (see diagram i). Center the plaited square and tighten. Then proceed by working around the square as in the first Square start, folding the four groups of four strands, each in its turn (see diagrams j, k, and l).

The final step in both of these starts is to stitch around the perimeter of the squares just created, using the binder to cover the four groups of foundation material and incorporate them into one resulting foundation bundle. To achieve this, thread the needle with an arm's length of binder, and at one corner (as close to the edge as possible) bring the needle through from the front of the start to the back, until all but the last inch of binder has passed through to the back. Laying this tail end with the foundation material directly to the left, bring the binder up in back (see diagram m) and over the top toward you; place the second stitch adjacent to the first (see diagram n). You will be stitching counterclockwise. Each of the four foundation groups will be added to the bundle in turn; the foundation bundle will reach its maximum size by the end of the first coil—one full turn around the square (see diagram o). After the first coil is completely stitched, the Square start is finished. The stitch may now be changed and a different foundation material may be substituted, if desired.

(We have labeled one side of the starts the "front" and the other side the "back," for the purpose of giving directions, but you may choose which side you want for front and back depending on which side you want to show on the inside and outside of the basket. See Orientation, page 14, for clarification.)

Second Square Start

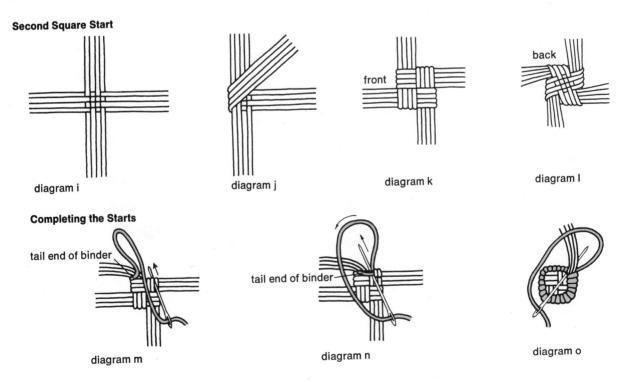

diagram i   diagram j   diagram k   diagram l

Completing the Starts

tail end of binder   tail end of binder

diagram m   diagram n   diagram o

Start for an Oval Basket

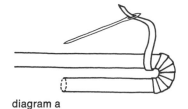

diagram a

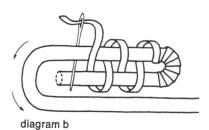

diagram b

START FOR AN OVAL BASKET

All oval-shaped baskets begin in much the same way, with slight variations caused by the basketmaker's choice of stitch. Select foundation material that is firm but not so rigid that it cannot be bent back on itself. Round reed (must be soaked for first one or two bends), cord, and rope are among those materials that are suitable. Bundles of finer materials may also be used, but with some loss of handling ease.

Bend foundation material at a point six or eight inches from one end. Hold it in the non-stitching hand, with the shorter part underneath and the bend close to the stitching hand. Lay the tail end of the binder on the short length, near the bend, and wrap to secure. Continue wrapping around the bend (see diagram a). Once the bend is rounded, hold the two lengths of the foundation firmly in the left hand while the other hand immediately begins to stitch along almost the entire length of the shorter part of the foundation (see diagram b). Use the Figure-Eight stitch as indicated in the diagram, as it offers greatest stability and complete coverage of foundation (a written description follows in the stitch section). Form a second bend so that the longer length of foundation bends around the shorter one, and wrap this bend with the binder until you are once again able to take a stitch. This completes the first coil and the Oval start. The stitch used may be changed at this point. On all succeeding bends, it will be possible to stitch coils together at all points, making unnecessary the wrapped bend of the first coil.

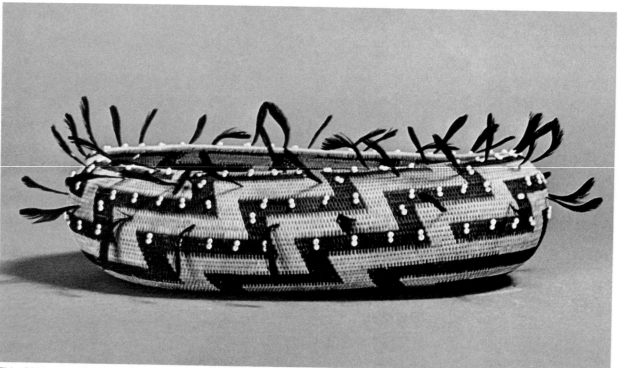

This 8½″ canoe basket, decorated with glass beads and feathers from the topknots of quails, is a striking example of Pomo Indian artistry. Photo by Carmelo Guadagno. Courtesy of the Museum of the American Indian, Heye Foundation. From the Judge Nathan Bijur Collection.

Central Knot Start for a Round Basket

diagram a

diagram b

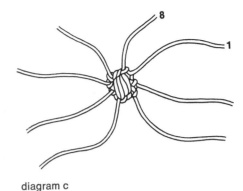

diagram c

CENTRAL KNOT START FOR A ROUND BASKET WITH A BUNDLE FOUNDATION

This type of start is taken from one used by the Pomo Indians of California. It is a small, tidy start giving the appearance of a single knot and suitable for flexible materials handled in small bunches.

Tie four strands of foundation (each eighteen inches long) together at the center into a firm, single overhand knot (see diagram a). Lay the eight resulting foundation ends out in a circle, and taking strands number 1 and number 8, tie a single overhand knot close to the side of the central knot (see diagram b). Moving in a counterclockwise direction, take strands 8 and 2, then 8 and 3, 8 and 4, 8 and 5, 8 and 6, 8 and 7, and finally 8 and 1 in turn, and tie each pair in an overhand knot, forming a ring of small knots around the central knot (see diagram c). Each knot must be pulled snugly next to the original center knot as it is made. Because one strand from the previous knot is always used with a new strand in forming each succeeding knot (the left-most strand is always number eight), the basketmaker cannot go back and retighten knots. Each knot is not a separate unit, but inextricably joined to those on each side of it.

To stitch, pull all eight strands slightly to the left of central knot (toward non-stitching hand) and hold them in this position with left hand. Thread needle with an arm's length of binder, and from front of start, bring needle through edge of central knot (barely catch fiber in central knot) toward the back until all but the last inch of binder has passed through. Lay the tail end of binder with the strands directly to the left of penetration (see diagram d). Proceed stitching counterclockwise around the circle of knots. Each stitch is taken to the left of and adjacent to the previous stitch. Each successive foundation strand is in turn incorporated with the previous ones until all eight strands constitute the foundation bundle. At this point, the Central Knot start is complete. A different type of material (such as cord, rope, or a bundle of less flexible material) may be substituted for the foundation bundle just created (see diagram e), and the stitch may be changed.

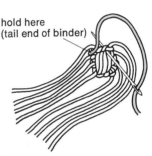

hold here (tail end of binder)

diagram d

new foundation

diagram e

Figure-Eight Stitch

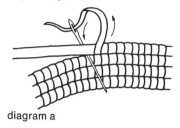

diagram a

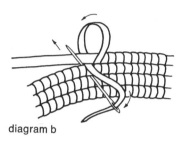

diagram b

Lazy Squaw Stitch

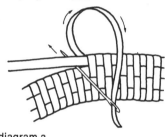

diagram a

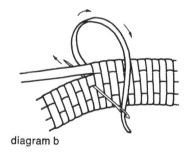

diagram b

Peruvian Stitch

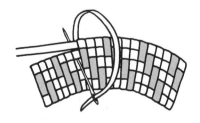

Stitches

As a rule, only two rows of foundation material are involved in stitching. (Some decorative stitches prove exceptions.) The *first row,* sometimes referred to as the *top row,* is the working, or new, foundation—the coil not yet covered by the binder. The *second row,* sometimes referred to as the *bottom row,* denotes the preceding row—the coil already covered by the binder and to which the first, or top, row will be secured by stitching. Consult the diagrams for clarification as you proceed.

FIGURE-EIGHT STITCH

This stitch is the most stable of all and should be used with this attribute in mind. If the procedure is followed unaltered, it allows a maximum number of stitches for joining the two coils involved, for there is no wrapping (covering only the working foundation with binder). Each coil is covered *two* times with binding material—once when it is the top row, and again, the next time around the basket, when it is the bottom row.

To stitch, bring threaded needle up from behind, *toward* you, between the previous coil and the new foundation. Wrap *away* from you, over the top of the new foundation, and bring the binder up between the new foundation and the previous coil, *toward* you, as before (diagram a). Carry the binder down around the *previous* coil and between stitches, and bring it up *toward* you, as before (diagram b). Continue stitching in this manner. To speed up construction, the stitches can be alternated with one, two, or three wraps around the working foundation only; however, the resulting basket will not be as sturdy.

LAZY SQUAW STITCH

This stitch gives a pleasing dovetailed appearance. Its unfortunate name derives from the action of alternating the stitch with the easier and faster motion of a wrap.

Coming from behind the working foundation, wrap the binder once around the working foundation (top row) *toward* you. Bring the binder up in back to complete the first step, a short wrap (see diagram a). Again, coming from behind the working foundation, bring the binder *toward* you, but this time carry the binder down around the *previous* coil (bottom row) to make a long stitch (see diagram b). With needle at original position at back of work, take up any slack in binder. Continue stitching in this manner. *Note:* Try to place each long stitch so that it covers the wrap below it on the previous coil.

PERUVIAN STITCH

The Peruvian stitch is really an extension of the Lazy Squaw: its long stitches are formed in exactly the same way. However, the space between stitches is increased by wrapping the top row two or three times between long stitches. In addition, the long stitches are most often placed directly to one side of those of the previous coil, with an eye to the radiating design they create (indicated by the tone in the diagram at left).

MARIPOSA STITCH

This stitch creates a lacy basket that has a definite preferred side: the one that shows the knots to best advantage.

Hold the working foundation about one-fourth inch from previous coil, and with the binder coming from behind the working foundation, bring it over the top *toward* you and wrap the working foundation. Now with binder again coming from behind the working foundation and over the top toward you, carry the binder over both the working foundation and the previous coil, then up through the space between them (see diagram a). Bring the binder horizontally from left to right across the long stitch just formed, and bring the needle up in back (see diagram b). A "knot" will have been formed. Continue stitching in this manner.

SAMOAN STITCH

This stitch is a variation of the Mariposa that leaves larger spaces between stitches and coils. Though the speed of fabrication is increased, the resulting basket is not as sturdy.

Follow the instructions for the Mariposa stitch. At the point where the binder is brought horizontally across the stitch to create the knot, repeat this wrapping motion several times to enlarge either the knot itself and/or the space between coils. (If the wraps are built up directly on top of each other, the knot will be enlarged; if they are taken in more of a side-by-side position, the space between coils will be enlarged as well.) The needle is then brought up in back, and the binder wraps the top row several times in order to increase the space between knots.

PLAIN STITCH

This stitch is particularly appropriate for use with a penetrable foundation bundle. Basketmakers also use it when coils of different colors are desired, because there is little overlap of binder onto the previous coil. The spaces between the stitches illustrated are shown only for clarification. In fact, stitches may completely cover the foundation.

The binder moves over the top of the working foundation *away* from you; a stitch is created by piercing the previous coil between stitches (diagram a) or by passing the needle under only the binder of the previous coil (diagram b). The latter technique is frequently used when the foundation material is difficult to penetrate, as with round reed. For other stitch variations, see the Harvey book listed in the Bibliography.

OPENWORK STITCHES

These various stitches are used when the basketmaker wishes to expose some of the foundation material. Often they are done simply to speed up the rate of fabrication; however, they also reveal the beauty and texture of some materials, as with pine needles, and the aroma, as with sweetgrass, of others. The textural pattern is most effective when the stitches are spaced evenly and when new stitches are added with an eye to the symmetry of the basket. Raffia openwork stitches on pine needles were used in the lovely covered basket, shown at right, from the Coushatta tribe of Louisiana. *Note:* See the Tod book listed in the Bibliography on page 64 for stitch instructions.

Mariposa Stitch

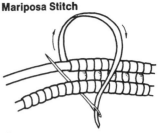

diagram a

diagram b

Plain Stitch

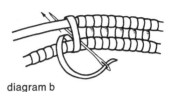

diagram a

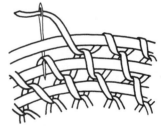

diagram b

Openwork stitches on pine needles

Splicing

The skill of splicing, or invisibly joining together, the ends of separate materials is a necessity in all basketry and particularly for coiling. For, in coiling, it is most convenient to work with only an arm's length of the binding material at one time; in addition, the length of the foundation is sometimes determined by the material's natural growth or ease of handling. For example, willow saplings are not of a continuous length, and when using heavy sisal rope as a foundation, the basketmaker may well find a length of rope more portable than the entire cone or ball.

SPLICING THE FOUNDATION

Fiber (single strand of several plies). In order to splice a foundation consisting of a single strand of yarn or rope, it is first necessary to taper the ends of both the old and new strands: untwist the plies for one inch and then cut off enough plies from each strand so that, in all, only the original number remains. Then hold the ends one against the other and twist to form a single unit once again (see photo on facing page). It may be advisable to secure the new foundation to the old by wrapping with sewing thread or even gluing. Always hold the spliced area securely until it is stitched over with the binder.

Susan Aaron-Taylor's "Ponca City Woman," 14" high, illustrates an imaginative use of shape and color in coiling. The detail below shows the right eye. Photos by Harry William Taylor.

Reeds. Small reeds should be spliced by cutting them bluntly and allowing them to meet end-to-end; large reeds may be cut obliquely over a space of one inch and laid one over the other with the circumference remaining constant. Hold securely until stitched in place.

Foundation bundles. Regardless of material selected (yarn, raffia, cord, grasses), foundation bundles must be kept at an even thickness to maintain uniform coils. Plan to add material only two or three strands at a time throughout the coiling process to avoid the bulge caused by adding a large number of strands all at once. If necessary, cut some strands before they run out in order to follow this pattern of staggered material addition.

SPLICING THE BINDER

The spliced binder is least discernible when splicing is accomplished during the wrapping rather than the stitching movement. Splicing can be performed in several ways. Two methods are described below:

1. Wrap foundation once with the old binder, and holding the tail ends (about one-and-a-half inches each) of both the old and new binders against the foundation and adjacent to the last wrap, wrap once around with the new binder to secure. Stitch as before. (See diagram a.)

2. Lay the tail end of the new binder along the foundation, and to secure it, continue stitching over both with the old binder for one inch. Wrap once with the old binder, then exchange the two, laying the tail end of the old binder against the foundation and wrapping over it with the new binder (see diagram b). Stitch as before.

Design Elements

DESIGN

In coiled baskets, design may be created in texture and color. While textural designs are limited by the nature of the materials and the stitches chosen, design possibilities in color and pattern are almost limitless, being restricted only by the impossibility of achieving a truly curved line or a closed circle. Because of the nature of the stitches, designs in coiled basketry are mostly geometric, although occasional representations of people and animals may be found (see photo on page 44). It is best to use small, discontinuous areas of pattern and to remember that the movement of the basket is spiral—horizontal stripes that cover an entire coil will never have a smooth join.

Other factors must be taken into account: the change in coil size due to shaping; the overlapping of colors inherent in some stitches, such as the Figure-Eight; and the nature of the material—dull, glossy, smooth, or fibrous.

There are those who prefer designing as the materials and their moods dictate, but for those who choose to plan a design in advance, it will help to work it out on graph paper, allotting one square to each stitch.

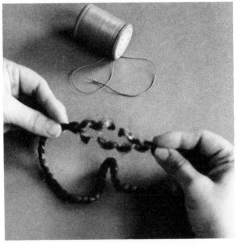

Splicing a 2-ply rope foundation. The ends were untwisted, and one ply was cut from each, so that only the original number of plies remains to be twisted together.

Splicing the Binder

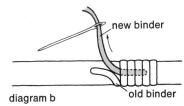

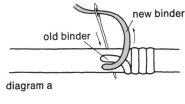

diagram a

diagram b

Note that in each method, the ends of both the old and the new binder will be completely covered by wrapping.

COLOR

Since several binders used at one time may become entangled, it is generally not advisable to create a design for a coiled basket with more than four colors in any one coil. It will be necessary for the basketmaker to carry all colors not in use along with the working foundation and to cover them totally with the binder. The color may be changed in much the same manner that a new binder is added on: take the color needed from the foundation bundle during a wrap movement, or wrap once with the old color, and holding the tail ends of both the old and new colors against the foundation and adjacent to the last wrap, wrap once around with the new color to secure (see diagram a on page 23).

SHAPE

Of all the basketry techniques, coiling permits the greatest freedom in shaping, for the contour, like the pattern, can change continuously as the basket is being made.

The contour of a coiled basket results from the precise placement of the foundation coils as the basket is being stitched, and is greatly influenced by the size and shape of the basket's base as well as by the materials used. These, in turn, are determined by the intended function of the basket. At the risk of oversimplifying, one may say that form follows function. A basket designed to hold large, heavy fruit should not have a small base and a tall stem leading to a sudden flare at the rim, nor should it use soft knitting yarn as binder or wool roving (unspun fleece) as foundation.

Whether round or oval, as a base grows in size, it becomes necessary to increase the number of stitches and/or wraps in each successive coil. The placement of these increases should be carefully made, in order to maintain the symmetry of the textural pattern. Sometimes it may be necessary to stitch or wrap twice or three times in the space where, just one coil before, only one stitch or wrap was needed.

When the appropriate base size has been achieved, it is time to begin bringing up the wall or sides of the basket. Generally, the basket is worked with the outside of the base *facing* the basketmaker to allow work on the outside of the basket; however, the method of working can be changed as the shape of the basket dictates (see Orientation, page 14). If the wall is to be built perpendicular to the base, lay the first foundation coil of the wall directly on *top* of the last coil of the base (see diagram a). Each successive coil can maintain this angle. If the circumference is to increase, lay each new coil on top of the preceding coil and to the *outside* of it (see diagram b). Use pressure from the non-stitching hand to help achieve the desired shape. To decrease the circumference, lay each coil on top but to the *inside* of the previous coil (see diagram c).

The contour line need not remain constant. The basketmaker may vary the placement of the coils a number of times in one basket as a means of achieving an unusual silhouette, a goblet stem, a narrow throat, or a flared rim. Open areas can be achieved by wrapping long lengths of the new foundation before restitching it to the previous row. Care should be taken to always keep the basket's function in mind when doing such experimenting.

Placement of Coils for Various Contours

a. Sides perpendicular to base

b. An increasing circumference

c. A decreasing circumference

Each circle in the diagrams above represents a foundation unit.

Finishing a Coiled Basket

The way in which the rim of a coiled basket is finished may greatly affect the basket's beauty and strength. Here we include three methods, starting with the simplest, for completing a coiled basket.

ABRUPT FINISH

This method works best in baskets made with a jute foundation and yarn or raffia binder; it lends to the basket an organic or primitive air.

Cut the foundation bluntly about one-half inch beyond the last stitch, and if it is jute or yarn, fray the edge. To secure the binder, draw the needle back through the foundation for one inch (see photo), bring it to the surface, and cut the binder as close to the basket as possible.

GRADUATED FINISH

When done well, this method gives the basket a neat, smooth rim capable of holding a lid and aesthetically very pleasing. (See bottom photo.)

Gradually decrease the diameter of the foundation over the last several inches of stitching until the width of the working foundation is very small (cut off plies one at a time for a yarn or jute foundation; shave down reed with a sharp blade; reduce the number of elements in the foundation bundle). Include this minimized foundation with the previous coil and make the last few stitches very secure. Run the needle back through the coil for about one inch and cut the excess binder.

DECORATIVE FINISHES

In addition to a graduated finish, described above, the basketmaker may wish to include a row of decorative stitching for color contrast or design interest or simply to strengthen the rim. If color contrast is desired, change binders and stitch over the last coil a second time; a different stitch may be used. Then bind off as before. Stitches commonly associated with embroidery may be adapted for special design effect.

Handles

STRUCTURAL

The following method is most effective for creating horizontal handles, although it can be adapted to create vertical ones.

At the point where the handle is desired, wrap the foundation coil and *extend* it out beyond the previous coils (and side) of the basket for the length of the handle. (You are, in effect, simply making a coil of a larger circumference than the rest of the basket.) The next coil may follow the contour of the handle coil and be stitched to it (if you want a thicker handle) or it may follow the contour of the previous basket coils. If a foundation bundle is being used, some additional material may be added for the length of the handle in order to increase stability; however, care must be taken lest the result appear bulky and awkward.

Abrupt finish, with needle in place to secure binder

Completed graduated finish

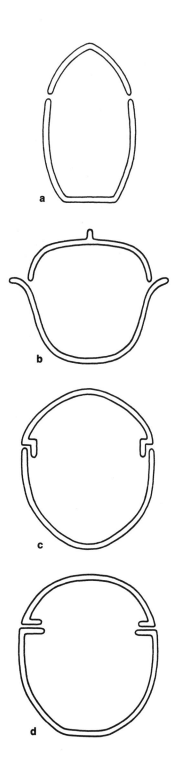

While this method does create a small open area in the side of the basket, thus making the basket unsuitable for carrying some small items, the handles are quite stable. If you want to avoid an open area, you may wish to use the following alternate method. Supplementary material for the handle is added to the foundation coil, and then *only* this new material is extended beyond the wall of the basket. Stitching continues on the original foundation material, and the handle is simply wrapped with additional binder. If you choose this method, make sure the handle is anchored firmly to the wall of the basket.

For vertical handles, the first method described is employed, but the wrapped area of foundation that will form the handle is drawn up and over the basket to the opposite side. There it is secured by stitching. It is difficult to continue coiling after forming a vertical handle, and if the basket is completed with a graduated finish soon after this point, the basket handle may not be secure enough for carrying a heavy load.

NONSTRUCTURAL

Using this method, vertical handles can be formed and, when worn out, may be easily replaced; however, since the handles are not part of the basket's structure, some strength is sacrificed.

When the basket is completed, form the handles separately from the same or different materials. Materials may be wrapped or braided to form handles that harmonize with the design of the basket. Attach by stitching or lashing to the basket diagonally across the join in an X-shape.

Lids

The shape of lids may be as varied as their basket counterparts. They are constructed in the same manner and can be made to fit baskets in several ways (see diagram). It is important that lids fit their baskets properly, be easy to handle, and be aesthetically pleasing and in proportion to the rest of the basket. Experimentation and experience will provide the essential information.

Lids on coiled baskets may (a) simply meet the basket edge-to-edge, (b) sit on a lip formed by the last few rows of the basket, (c) have a ledge that fits inside the edge of the basket, or (d) have a ledge that sits on another ledge formed by the last few rows of the basket. Other variations are also possible.

This African disc, 12″ in diameter, is an excellent example of the use of color in coiled basketry. Note the detail at the disc's edge.

Construction Techniques: Woven Basketry (Twining, Plaiting, Wickerwork)

The subtle texture of the goatskin lacing is the focal point of Nancy Bess's simple twined baskets.

Some of the most exciting and unusual basketry in the world is constructed using traditional weaving techniques. Among the pieces are those not generally included under the heading of *basket*—fans, sieves, hats, and brooms.

In coiled basketry, shaping is fluid and dependent upon the placement of the foundation and the manner of stitching; in woven basketry there is a preset substructure created by the arrangement of warps at the base. Of course, some variation is possible, but, for the most part, woven baskets are more rigid than coiled in the way they define space. In addition, the major tools of woven basketry are the hands; no stitching is necessary.

This chapter will present the manner of constructing woven baskets by twining, plaiting, and wickerwork: different ways of starting; different weaves; how to handle color, design, and shaping; and methods of finishing the baskets, including the addition of handles and lids.

Cane is the primary material in these wickerwork and plaited baskets from Colombia.

GLOSSARY

Warp(s) (also called spokes)—the stiff foundation elements that constitute the structure of the basket and around which the weaving takes place. The warps are generally larger and less flexible than the weft material.

Weft(s) (also called weavers)—the flexible material that is manipulated around the warps of a basket in a variety of patterns.

Twining—a basketry technique in which the warps are held in place by two or more flexible wefts that are twisted, or crossed, between warp strands or groups of warp strands. The type of crossing that is most often used is referred to as a half-twist (see page 36). Both round and flat materials may be used in twining.

Plaiting—a woven basketry technique in which the warp and weft are indistinguishable from one another; that is, they are of equal width and equally functional and active. Only flat material is used, and a wide variety of patterns is possible.

Checkerwork—sometimes used as a synonym for plaiting; here it refers only to plaiting in the over-one, under-one pattern, using materials of equal width.

Wickerwork—a basketry technique in which a single weft passes over and under successive warps; round materials are generally used, but flat materials are also appropriate. The weft is traditionally smaller and more flexible than the warp.

Splintwork—a woven basketry technique in which the materials are limited to those that are flat, and sometimes more specifically to splint; the width of the weft can be equal to or smaller than the width of the warp.

Plain Weave—a textile term referring to a type of weave in which the weft always moves in the over-one, under-one pattern; bears no relationship to materials used. Because of the high number of intersections produced between warp and weft, plain weave is very stable and serviceable.

Woody Material—a nontechnical term applied here to those natural and commercially prepared materials that are relatively inflexible and woodlike when dry; includes, for our purposes, splint, round and flat reed, cane, vines, runners, and willow.

Materials

The selection of materials for woven baskets is a process very similar to that for coiled work—form and function both affect the material selection, and, correspondingly, if certain materials are desired, the type of basket possible or suitable is then determined.

The elements in twining and wickerwork can be examined together, for though they are entirely separate techniques, they are not unrelated. In both, the warps must be strong enough to support the weft and to create the basket's skeletal or foundation system.

Willow is the traditional natural material used; however, it is not now easily available and does involve both a storage problem and a curing process. Round reed is a popular choice since it can be purchased from a number of mail-order suppliers. It is inexpensive and already completely processed. Shipped in bundles, it need only be soaked before use. For those who prefer a more contemporary look or a firm but less rigid basket, jute cord and rope are often used. These last items are available everywhere, easily stored, and require no further preparation. They have an additional advantage for those involved in textile crafts, as they can be used in other fiber projects.

Upon casual glance, it would seem that the weft in these baskets is less significant structurally than the warp, in that it is not part of the support system of the basket; however, this is not the case. The weft material determines the spacing and position of the warps and maintains them in their desired position. Baskets that have identical warp material but use different weft will vary not only in appearance but in stability and function as well.

When choosing weft material for more rigid baskets, again the natural and processed woody materials are often selected. The willow and round reed used for weft will be smaller, and thus more flexible, than those used for warp. Vines and runners are equally versatile as weft but include the same gathering and curing problems as the willow. For the less rigid, natural baskets, corn husks, bundles or braids of grasses, and leaves are frequently selected. They do not have the storage and curing problems of the larger natural materials (only drying is required).

Perhaps the most versatile of the fibers used are the yarns and cords. Widely available, they come in every conceivable color, texture, and finish. They have the added advantage over the more rigid materials of being easy to handle even when the weaver has no prior experience.

Plaiting presents problems particular to technique. You will find a narrower range of materials suitable, as they must by definition be flat and of equal size.

In selecting plaiting materials, think of the intended function and the desired size of the basket. For example, if the basket is to be used for carrying or will have any contact with water (as a flowerpot holder, perhaps), a woody material such as flat reed or splint might be the best choice.

Baskets of ribbon, fabric strips, or paper are more vulnerable to damage and are usually limited to decorative items. Paper is an especially helpful material for samples, as it holds a crease (at base where sides turn up) and saves on expense when experimenting. The traditional materials of yucca and palm, though not naturally available everywhere, are worth seeking out, for the baskets made of them are truly striking.

With all three techniques, it is helpful to work a small sample before cutting the material for the actual basket. The sample will give you the needed information regarding the flexibility and spacing of the warp and the weft, and you will be able to see how the materials you have chosen look together.

It cannot be stressed too strongly that practice and sample work are essential to proper material selection.

Starts

In woven basketry, the term *start* refers to the initial unit of weaving, which establishes the relationship of the warp and weft to each other. In some cases, the start may comprise the entire base and involve considerable weaving; in others, the warps are laid out initially in their proper relationship, with minimal weaving needed to define this relationship. Generally, you will be working on the *outside* of what will be the basket's base.

The descriptions that follow by no means exhaust the possibilities, but they are representative of the major types of woven basketry starts. Specific information regarding number of warps, length of materials, diameter of basket, etc., is included in order to clarify, by example, the technical descriptions. It is not intended to define specific projects, but rather, through sample work, to allow you to gain the experience and information necessary to begin woven basketry.

When choosing a start, first define the basket's function so the proper material can be selected. For example, if you want a simple, twined fiber basket to hold dried flowers, yarn weft on jute warp would be suitable. In turn, the start using overlapping squares works well with these materials and suits the function of the basket.

Over a period of time a weaver develops an eye for the quantity of material needed in basketry. Initially, though, measuring and the exercise of logic are required. With our example of the flower basket, first determine the size base and the height of the basket needed for the floral arrangement. Then cut several sample pieces of the jute warp and twine across them to determine the spacing of warps caused by twining with the specific yarn weft chosen. From this sample, the number of warps needed to make the desired base size can be computed. The warp material should then be cut long enough to cover the base and two sides, plus some extra for the rim and waste allowance. This simple, logical procedure of choosing the right material and estimating the proper quantity can be generalized to apply to other pieces.

Note: If you wish to add handles to your basket, consult the section on Handles (pages 42–43) for specific information before beginning the start for the basket. Generally, if the handles are to be structural, one usually cuts some warps (which will end up being the handles) longer than others. If the handles are to be nonstructural, then spaces for the handles are held open until the completion of the basket by means of sticks placed in the weaving.

SQUARE-BASE START—CHECKERWORK (flat material)

Using flat strips of material, cut ten pieces of equal length. Each strip should be long enough to cover the base, two sides, and about four inches of excess for the rim and waste. So, for a basket that will measure six inches across the base and eight inches in height, cut each warp twenty-six inches long (6 + 8 + 8 + 4). Remember to cut some warps longer if you want structural handles. *Note:* If using woody material such as ash

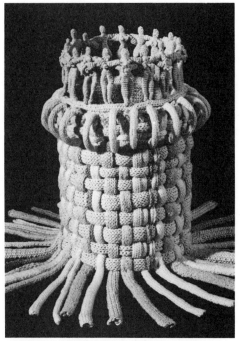

In Norma Minkowitz's basket form, "Around and Around," 14″ x 8″, knitted strips were woven in checkerwork for the sides, and the figures at the top were crocheted. Photo by Kobler/Dyer Studios.

Square-Base Start—Checkerwork

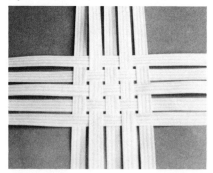

All ten strips interwoven, tightened, and centered, with quarter-inch spaces between strips

Overlapping Squares Start—Twining

Placing the weft around the warps

The first row of twining completed

Starting the second row of twining

splint, remember to soak for the appropriate length of time and to look for the smooth and rough sides. The smooth side should appear on the outside of the basket.

Lay five of the strips on a table, parallel to one another and one-quarter inch apart. Starting in the center area of the strips, begin weaving the other five strips one at a time among the five already on the table. The first strip will weave over one, under one, etc., and the second will weave just the opposite—under one, over one, etc. When all ten strips are interwoven, tighten and center the weave with your fingers, leaving the quarter-inch spaces. (See photo.)

It is helpful to bind base elements together before folding up the sides. Use a narrow strip of cane or reed, and weave around the perimeter, in and out of the spaces created by the checkerwork.

To prepare for weaving the sides, bend the spokes at a 90° angle to the table, along the perimeter of the base—bending the spokes up against a flat-edged ruler will help form a neat edge. Again, if using woody materials, make sure material is damp enough to bend without cracking.

RECTANGULAR-BASE START—CHECKERWORK (flat material)

If a rectangular base is desired, the procedure is the same as that for the Square-Base start, but an adjustment is made regarding the number of warps interwoven. A square base requires that the number of warps on each side be equal; a rectangular base requires an unequal number of warps. To make the rectangular shape more pronounced, have the number of warps of one direction markedly greater than those of the opposite direction. For example, a basket that is three warps by nine warps will readily appear rectangular, while one that is three warps by five warps may initially appear to be square.

OVERLAPPING SQUARES START—TWINING

For this start, which makes a round basket, two squares are twined and then laid one over another. A wide variety of materials is suitable, as long as the warp is sturdier and thicker than the weft. If a heavy yarn is desired for weft, then a sturdy jute or rope would be a suitable warp; if raffia is used as weft, then reeds might be used as warp. The number of strands used will vary according to the desired size of the base and the type and dimensions of the materials used. It should be noted, however, that when using very round, firm material for warp, the resulting base is quite bulky and the basket may not sit perfectly upright.

For our example, a basket whose base is about six inches and whose height is eight inches, cut two sets of eight strands each of warp material, each strand measuring twenty-six inches. Begin by holding one set of eight strands in the nonworking hand just below center or by laying the strands on a flat work surface. Then double a length of weft and place the doubled weft around the warps, with half the weft in front and the other half behind the warps, and the fold at the side of the warps farthest away from the working hand (see photo). Begin twining (see page 36) toward the working hand, a pair of warps at a time, to the end of the row (see photo). Flip the work over side-to-side so that the weft ends once again begin farthest away from the working hand, and again work toward it (see photo). At the end of the row, push the second row up against the first so that no warp is visible between the two rows. Continue twining until there is a square of work as long as it is wide and slightly smaller than the desired base size. Make a temporary slip knot or over-hand knot to secure.

Then form a second square, using the second set of eight strands of warp. This square will be laid on top of the first square and will be on the outside of the basket, so make it slightly longer, perhaps by two rows of twining, so that the warps will be covered when they are bent upwards to form the sides. Remember that you are twining on the *outside* of what will be the basket's base.

Lay the second square over the first so that eight warps radiate from each of the four sides and so that all four wefts are in the same corner (see photo). Using the wefts in pairs (one from the top and one from the bottom), continue twining around the squares until all thirty-two warps have been joined, thus uniting the two squares. Remember you are twining around pairs of warps. Then, after this first round of twining is completed, drop one weft from each pair and either draw the dropped ones through the weaving with a crochet hook or needle or let them hang to the underside of the base just created. A circular base will result unless the sides are turned up immediately after the joining of the two squares. (If a slightly larger, circular base is desired, only one warp at a time may be twined, and/or more warps may be added before turning up the sides.) Be careful to turn the sides up in the proper direction—you have been twining on the *outside* of the base and it must remain the outside! After doing so, continue twining the remaining pair of weft strands in a circular fashion.

OVERLAPPING SQUARES START—WICKERWORK

The structure of this base is exactly the same as that described for the twining start, and also produces a round basket. Again, two squares are formed and laid over one another. However, the weaving is done in wickerwork rather than in twining. A single weft is used and is woven over one, under one, across the set of warps until the desired size is reached. Make two squares and lay one square on top of the other, with the two wefts at one corner; twine *one* row around the entire set of warps to hold the squares together. At the end of the row, drop one weft strand and return to wickerwork. The sides will bend up automatically. Add material as needed, and change color as desired.

ROUND START—TWINING OR WICKERWORK

This start has many variations in the number of beginning warps and in the manner of lashing them together, but it is a basic, universal start for round twined and wickerwork baskets. For our example, cut eight eighteen-inch lengths of warp material and lay four lengths over and perpendicular to four others, at their center. (You can also cut small transverse slits through one set of four warps, at their central points, and pass the other four through the slits—see photo.) In either case, lash these warps together (see photo).

The second square laid over the first, with eight warps radiating from each of the four sides and all four wefts in the upper left-hand corner, ready for twining

Round Start—Twining or Wickerwork

One set of warps passing through transverse slits in other set

Warps lashed in place at center

Round Start—Radiating Spokes

Warps laid out in a radiating pattern

diagram a

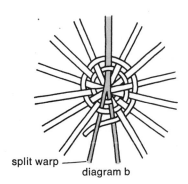

split warp ──────
diagram b

additional half-length warp ─┐

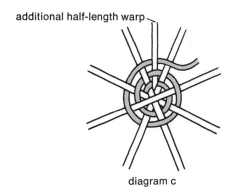

diagram c

ROUND START (RADIATING SPOKES)—TWINING OR WICKERWORK

Although splint of ash or oak was the traditional material used in this technique, other flat materials, such as cane, reed, and bark, are also suitable and produce much the same results. Weft material can range from sweet grass used in bundles or braids to reeds, cane, bark, or splint.

To begin, cut eight splints to measure (base plus two sides plus waste), and lay them in sequence and crisscrossing one another at their centers to form a radiating pattern. Leave equal spaces between warps (see photo). Weave a narrow weft under one, over one, taking each warp in sequence and pressing the weaving tight and as close to the center as possible. When one round is completed, the weaver has several options (see diagram): (a) Overlap the weft ends over and under a few warps and clip. Begin the second round with a new weft and at a different point on the circle for strength, weaving opposite the first round (that is, under one where the first round is over one), and overlapping the ends as before. Continue for entire diameter of base, using a new weft for each round. (b) Cut one warp in half lengthwise to center of basket, and press the halves apart; continue weaving with the same weft, but count the cut warp as two—the odd number that results will allow each round to be woven opposite to its predecessor. (c) Add one half-length splint to give an odd number of warps, and weave continuously with one weft. *Note:* We have given eight warps for our example, but in actuality you may use the number of warps that seems appropriate to the material you have chosen. For clarity, the diagrams show fewer warps than the photo.

(There are still other variations in the formation of this base—warps may be added or tapered to facilitate shaping, etc. Consult the Bibliography, page 64, for books specializing in this area of basketry.)

When the base is woven to its desired diameter, bend up the warp for the sides. (Be sure material is sufficiently damp to prevent cracking.) Bending the warps up over a circular form of the appropriate size (plate, bowl, etc.) may help to ensure proper base outline.

TWO STARTS FOR A FLAT, TWINED BAG OR POUCH

Twined bags may be started from the top and worked down or started from the bottom and worked up. Using the former method, it is necessary, when the bag is completed, either to knot the warp ends together at the bottom and leave a fringe or to sew the two sides of the bag together across the bottom. Twining up permits a finished bottom, but requires that all the warp ends be tucked in or sewn under at the top edge.

Starting at the Top. As this start requires mounting macramé knots on a holding cord, T-pins and an appropriate board—lightweight, firm, yet flexible enough for pins to be inserted—are helpful. Work can also be done on a flat surface, using masking tape in place of T-pins to secure the holding cord while working.

A doubled length of warp material will be used for the holding cord, and it should be cut to measure twice the circumference plus a few inches for waste. For example, if the circumference of the bag is to be twenty inches, a length of cord about forty-four inches must be cut. (The extra four inches may be used as a drawstring when the bag is completed.)

Cut warp lengths to measure twice the length of the bag plus waste allowance. (These lengths will be folded in half for mounting.) Secure doubled holding cord with pins to a board and begin mounting folded lengths of warp with Lark's Head macramé knots (see diagram). Each folded warp creates two warps when knotted on the holding cord. Add each warp length in the same manner, and push warps close together so that they entirely cover the holding cord.

When all the warps have been mounted, remove the holding cord from the board and tighten knots; tie the holding cord in a circle with an overhand knot. When twining from the top you may find it more comfortable to work with the knotted holding cord closest to you and the warps moving away from you. Begin twining at any point on the circumference and continue working around the circle—there will be no side seams at all.

Starting at the Bottom. Cut all the warps to twice the length of the bag plus waste allowance, and lay them parallel to one another. Twine one row across the center and flip over (side-to-side) as in the Overlapping Squares start for twining (see page 32). Twine two more rows in this manner, then fold the bag in half lengthwise along the center row of twining (the warps are now doubled over on themselves). From this point, twine in a circular path around the entire bag, taking each warp in turn. A variation of this start is used in a project (see page 57).

OVAL START—TWINING OR WICKERWORK

Woven baskets are not limited to round or square bases, though these are more frequently used. The basic Oval start is easily adapted to ovals of various proportions by simply increasing the number of warps going in one direction.

To begin, cut four strips of warp material to measure the *length* of the base plus two sides plus waste and another eight strips to measure the *width* of the base plus two sides plus waste. Pierce the short warps at their centers and thread the long warps through, making sure that the length from A to B equals that from B to C (see diagram a).

To begin twining, fold weft in half. Place doubled weft around four warps at one end (with half the weft in front of and the other half behind the warps). Twine for two rounds using sets of four warps as if they were one. On the third round of twining, use *two* warps as one, thus doubling the number of twining half-twists. On the fifth or sixth round, separate all the warps and twine singly. (See diagram b.) Put pressure on warps to form the oval, and be sure the weaving is tight. If you wish, when half the base in completed, reverse the direction of the twining in order to counteract the tendency for the oval base to twist. When the base is the desired size, bend up the warps and weave the sides.

For wickerwork, tuck the end of a single weaver to what will be the inside of the basket and begin weaving in the over-one, under-one pattern characteristic of wickerwork. The spacing of the warps may differ from that of the twining version and the sides may come up more abruptly, depending on the material you have chosen. Twining and wickerwork may, of course, be combined. For example, use twining until the warps can be worked singly, and then change to wickerwork.

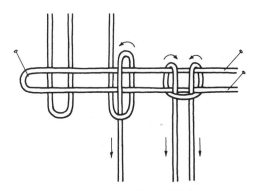

Mounting warps on a doubled holding cord with Lark's Head macramé knots

Oval Start—Twining or Wickerwork

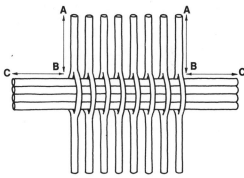

diagram a

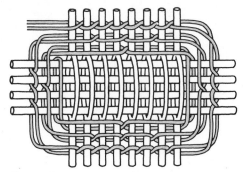

diagram b

Twining sets of four warps as one, two warps as one, and single warps. *Note:* For clarity, only three rows of twining are shown in the diagram. Refer to the text for the correct number of rounds to twine each set. When twining, the space at the corners will begin to close up, and the base will assume an oval shape.

Checkerwork

2/2 twill

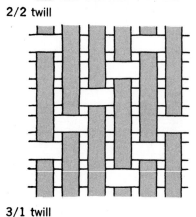

3/1 twill

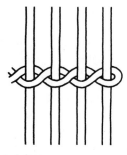

Plain twining

Weaves

CHECKERWORK

Checkerwork is a plain-weave technique often used in splint basketry; it involves the weaving of flat strips of material—all the same size—over and under each other (see diagram). The first two weavers are difficult to weave and often slip out of place. It may be helpful for the beginner to use clothespins to hold ends in place until the sides are well supported. The first weft that forms the sides should be woven opposite to the last weft of the base.

If the weft is relatively narrow (less than one-half inch), and the warps are of an *uneven* number, the sides may be worked in a continuous spiral. Taper the weft ends over an inch or so and overlap them only when the weft has run out. Alternately, the sides may be woven row by row, with each row using a separate piece of weft (here, the warps can be of an *even* number). The overlapping weft ends should be placed at varying points around the circumference to avoid weakening the structure. The ends are always set on the inside of the basket, and the overlapping areas may be shaved so that the thickness of the weft remains constant.

TWILLS—PLAITING AND WICKERWORK

Twills are used in wickerwork and plaiting to create surface interest, to display color, and to add strength and durability. A twill is created when the weaver passes over and under the spokes in any combination other than the over-one, under-one of Plain weave. In deciding whether to use a twill, the basketmaker must consider the nature of the materials and the function of the basket. The long floats of material sometimes created would be undesirable in a basket that receives constant and heavy handling. The weave must be staggered at the beginnings of the rows so that the pattern doesn't simply line up. Two twill variations are shown in the diagrams at left.

PLAIN TWINING

This is a technique in which two wefts cross each other between warps (or between groups of warps) creating a half-twist at each crossing (see diagram). Each weft alternately appears on the inside and then on the outside of the basket as work moves in a spiral from the base to the top of the basket. New weft is added as needed (see Splicing, page 39).

Plain twining may be done as *closed work,* with each row forced directly adjacent to the previous row and, therefore, covering the warps entirely; or as *openwork,* with each row separate from its predecessor, thus exposing warp material. Openwork is often used in combination with Plain weave or with crossed warps for special effects (see project on pages 57–58).

To begin, fold a length of weft material in half (thus creating two weft lengths), slip the fold down around a warp, and start twining.

Plaiting is the predominant weaving technique used in these collection samples, which represent a wide range of basketry functions.

TWILLED, OR DIAGONAL, TWINING

Diagonal twining is so called because it creates a diagonal groove across the weft. This technique is always worked on an odd number of warps that are twined two at a time. At the end of the first row, therefore, the last unworked warp will be twined along with the first warp of the first pair, splitting the pair. Each pair thereafter will be split, as well. After several rows of twining, the diagonal line becomes obvious.

THREE-STRAND TWINING

This strong weave is often used on the bottom of a basket, around the crown of a hat where base and sides meet, or just as a decorative band. Three wefts are used simultaneously. Each one passes *over* two warps and *under* one so that the inside has the appearance of single plain twining, while the outside maintains the appearance particular to this technique (see diagram). When an area of Three-strand twining is desired, cut a third piece of weft and insert tail end into weaving to secure. *Note:* There will always be a short section where the weaving must be adapted to the new pattern of twining—some of the wefts must make "floats" to achieve the correct relationship of wefts to each other in the over-two, under-one pattern. Diagram will clarify.

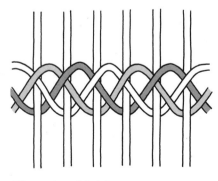

Three-strand twining

This detail of Susan Goldin's disc reveals her use of openwork twining with manipulation of warps. The entire disc is pictured on page 64. Photo by Steve Anderson.

Susan Aaron-Taylor's 3½′ high "Pod Environment" illustrates the subtle but dramatic shaping possible with twining even in works of this scale. Photo by Harry William Taylor.

Splicing

Splicing materials in woven basketry is, for the most part, a matter of common sense; often it involves simply overlapping beginnings and endings on the interior of the basket and staggering these weak spots in the weave. However, some additional information may be helpful for the beginner when dealing with weft materials.

Especially in twined work, splicing has some variations. A single strand may be spliced by overlapping the new and old ends for two or three half-twists and then placing the ends to the inside of the basket. If both wefts are to be replaced at the same time, a process similar to beginning the twining (see twining diagram, page 36) can be used. Fold the new length of weft material in half, and slip the fold down around the warp where weft has ended. Half the weft will be in front of the warp and half behind. Continue twining with this new weft and leave tail ends of replaced weft behind, to be dealt with later. *Note:* Some additional bulk is created when using this technique. It is suggested that weft pieces generally be spliced separately (at different places).

At times, it is necessary to further conceal the ends of material for reasons of aesthetics and stability. To do this, thread weft end on needle, place needle parallel to warp, and slip under several rows of twining. Pull excess to surface and clip. This is especially simple when working with yarn or jute weft. For more rigid material, use an awl to create a space under twining rows.

Design Elements

COLOR

In wickerwork and twining, color and design go hand-in-hand. Colored materials are added by splicing and help achieve variations in weave or in the overall appearance of a basket. Care should be taken to choose a weave that shows dyed materials to their best advantage and to use naturally dyed materials frugally.

Twining offers even more design variations than wickerwork with regard to the use of color. To create vertical stripes, two different colored wefts may be used on an even number of warps; the same color will always fall on the same warp. Alternately, two different colored wefts may be used on an odd number of warps to create a small checkerboard or spiral stripe appearance. The same effect can be achieved with an even number of warps by making one full twist between two warps at the end of each full round (rather than a half-twist), thus changing the color sequence.

SHAPE

Although changing the shape of woven baskets is not as simple as changing that of coiled (indeed, the shaping of a twined basket is a difficult enterprise), variation is possible if one adjusts tension, changes the size or number of warps, or alters the weft material.

Gary Trentham's extraordinary craftsmanship and sense of design are immediately evident in his cotton rope basket, 38″ in diameter and 11″ deep. The piece was coiled from base to curved edge, and then additional material was added and knotted with half-hitches. Photo by John P. Creel III.

As in coiling, the contours of a woven basket are greatly influenced by the size and shape of the base and by the materials used; these, in turn, are determined, for the most part, by the function of the basket.

For all woven baskets, the silhouette will tend to bulge outward when the weaving is loose, and conversely, it will decrease in diameter when the weavers are being pulled tightly. Guard against accidental changes in shape, but utilize these tension principles when such changes are desired.

For those who find it difficult to control tension, a more efficient and predictable way of varying contour is to alter the number of spokes. The simplest method for achieving this is to cut new spokes and insert them as needed. Another method is to divide some of the existing warps (or groups of warps) and increase the number of twining half-twists accordingly. To simplify this last method, you may want to work with groups of warps divisible by two. For example, work twining around groups of four warps until the point where an increase in circumference is desired. Then, twine around groups of two warps. The number of weft half-twists in one round is thus doubled, and because they occupy extra space, the circumference is accordingly expanded. An additional increase can be achieved by eventually twining around a single warp.

Regardless of the technique used to increase the circumference, take care lest the basket develop asymmetrically.

To decrease the diameter in a twined or wickerwork basket, warps previously woven singly can be paired. Alternately, some warps may be eliminated, or, particularly in baskets made of flat material, the warps can be tapered and the pressure of the weaver maintained to diminish the contour.

Finishing a Woven Basket

TWINING

Abrupt Finish. This is the simplest method for finishing a twined basket and is effective with reeds or fibers. Simply cut the warp off even with the edge of the basket. (Sometimes Diagonal or Three-strand twining can be used for the last row to form a small ridge.) This method is best limited to those baskets in which the edge is protected or will receive little stress.

A variation of this finish is to have the last few rows differ in weave from the rest of the basket and then to cut the warp off a short distance beyond the finish, leaving a kind of fringe. For example, a diagonal-twined basket may have a border of plain twining. If the warp is fibrous, such as a multiple-ply jute, this finish can be exaggerated by leaving more warp exposed—separate the plies and fray the fibers into a brushlike fringe (see photo on page 2).

Folding Warps Down on Themselves. Used also in plaited and wickerwork baskets, all variations of this method provide a neat edge, which can include a fancy braid if desired.

The simplest way of doing this is to taper the warp ends, fold the warp back on itself at the very edge of the weaving, then pass over the last twined row and slip the tapered ends back through a few woven rows of the basket (see diagram). Clip remaining ends. For fibers, a crochet hook will be of use; for stiffer materials, an awl will help lift the weft for the warp to pass under. This procedure is usually done on the interior of the basket, where it is least visible.

Folding Warps Down on Other Warps. For variation, warps may be folded down not on themselves, but next to adjacent warps or warps that are farther away, and then bound in place with one or more rows of twining (see diagram). To facilitate this process, the warp ends should be long enough to fold over and still allow easy movement of the fingers among them. After the twining is completed, pull the warp ends firmly into place, leaving no loops of warp above the woven area.

Scalloped Edge. Also used in plaiting and wickerwork. To form a scalloped edge, simply take each warp in turn (precut to four inches beyond the last row of weaving and tapered), wet it if necessary, and curve it toward the right or left. Tuck each warp two inches into the weaving at a point at least two warps to the right (or left) of itself (see diagram).

PLAITING AND WICKERWORK

Forming and Reinforcing a Rim. When the walls of the basket have reached their required height, form a rim in the following manner. Use your fingers or an awl to push all the weaving close together, one row directly on top of the other. To make reinforcement rims, cut two lengths of splint (or similar material), each four inches longer than the circumference of the top of the basket, and soak in warm water. They will be used later. Cut off every warp that has ended on the *inside* of the basket during the final row of weaving, as close as possible to that last row. Leave a three-inch excess on all the warps that are on the *outside* of the final row of weaving. Trim this last group of warps to a point. Keeping the warps damp, bend them over the final row of weaving (and close to it) toward the inside of the basket, and push them into the weave so that they do not show (see diagram).

Now add the reinforcement rims. Place one along the inside edge—natural pressure will hold it in place—and one along the outside. Use clothespins to hold the latter in place. Stagger the endings of these rims, and shave the edges so that when the ends overlap they remain one splint thick. Lash the rims into place with a reed, a length of cane, a long thin splint pointed at one end, or yarn (see diagram). Place the stitches in the spaces between warps and wefts; use an awl to enlarge these spaces, if necessary. Do not twist binder. When the entire circumference is lashed in place, overlap by one or two stitches, tuck the end under some of the stitches, and clip the excess. For a more decorative method of lashing, see the photos on page 63.

Decorative and Braided Borders for Wickerwork. Many decorative and braided borders have been invented for wickerwork baskets. Refer to the books listed in the Bibliography (page 64) for a fuller treatment of the subject.

Folding warps down on themselves

Folding warps down on other warps

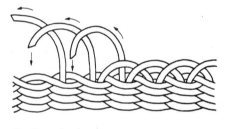

Scalloped edge

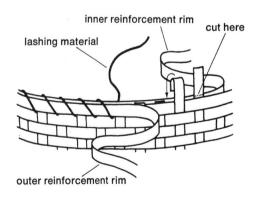

inner reinforcement rim

cut here

lashing material

outer reinforcement rim

Forming and reinforcing a rim

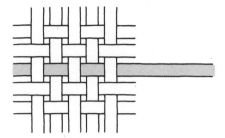

Middle warp left longer on one side

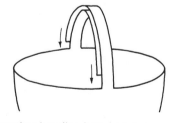

Inserting handle into weaving

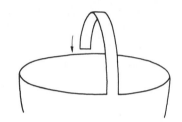

Middle warp left longer on both sides

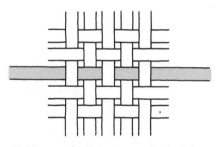

Inserting handles into weaving

Handles

As with coiled basketry, handles may be structurally included when making a woven basket or they may be added on after the basket's completion. An ambitious basketmaker may carve handles. Others may prefer to purchase handles or fashion them from gathered or purchased materials.

Regardless of materials and techniques used, it is strongly suggested that samples be experimented with prior to making final decisions on an actual project. This experimentation allows the basketmaker to develop a sense of the aesthetic questions involved—the weight and height of the handle in relationship to the bulk of the basket, the degree of refinement appropriate for materials used—as well as some practical knowledge in handling materials for this specific purpose.

STRUCTURAL

These handles are frequently created by intentionally cutting some warps longer than others at the start, thereby having handle materials ready when the top of the basket is reached. Usually the central warp of the warps going in one direction is left longer (see diagrams). When the top is reached, handle material can be bent to the opposite side of the basket and inserted into the weaving (see diagrams). Or, by bringing materials from two directions (opposite sides) and wrapping them together into a single unit, a sturdy, functional handle can be easily made.

NONSTRUCTURAL

It is most common to find handles that have been added on to plaited and wickerwork baskets; this is not to say that when weaving these baskets the craftsperson needn't make any adjustments for these handles. On the contrary, spaces for the attachment of handles are held open until the basket is completely woven with sticks of the same or slightly smaller size placed several inches down into the weaving. The sticks are then removed and replaced by the handles. If this were not done, the tightly woven wefts would break or be placed under great tension when the handles were inserted and the shape of the basket possibly distorted.

HANDLES FOR SPLINT BASKETS

The handles most typically used for splint baskets are rigid ones, often carved from the same material as that used to construct the basket. Sometimes grooves that are the width of the basket's rim reinforcements are carved into the handle so that a bulge will not be created by the rim when the handles are inserted.

HANDLES FOR WICKERWORK BASKETS

With some exceptions, wickerwork baskets usually have handles that have been added onto the structure. These handles may be braided or twisted groupings of the material used to construct the basket, or they may be plaited bands of leather or other materials; all should be attached to the basket in an attractive and durable fashion. The ends of the handles must be tapered and inserted well into the weaving, where sticks have been maintaining a space for them. Some basketworkers may wish to leave it at that; however, for greater stability, the handles may also be lashed to the basket.

The Twisted Handle. Commonly used with wickerwork baskets, this handle is easy to make but suitable only for those baskets not used for carrying. Cut and taper two presoaked lengths of handle material such as willow or round reed, and place both ends securely into one of the spaces maintained by the substitute stick. To twist the material lengths around one another, place one piece in each hand and exchange hands repeatedly and with even pressure until only three or four inches of material remain untwisted. Insert these remaining two ends into the space at the other side of the basket, and secure both sides with small nails if necessary. For a heavier handle, a greater number of rods may be used. See the photo at right for one of the variations possible with twisted handles.

The Wrapped Handle. This technique is really a decorative one, as it merely covers the handle with a secondary material. The easiest method simply involves laying one strand of flat material on the top surface of the handle while a second strand wraps both the decorative strip and the handle together. The second strand can wrap behind this decorative material at regular intervals to create a simple embellishment similar to that created by the "beading" technique used in coiling (see page 45). The handle is attached to the basket in the same manner as in the previous description.

HANDLES FOR TWINED BASKETS

Traditional twined baskets show handles very infrequently, and, when they do, the handles are usually strips of leather or woven material that are attached to the basket by stitching or tying after the basket has been completed. Occasionally, large twined baskets, such as those from Ethiopia that are sold in American markets today, show sturdy handles wrapped with the same material used in the construction of the basket.

Lids

In plaited, twined, and wickerwork baskets, lids are constructed precisely as if a new basket were to be made, but the dimensions are more critical and are based on those of the companion basket. The lid can be a separate shallow or domed basket of the proper size and shape to fit just over the outside of the rim. Where there are handles, the lid should be just smaller than the inside size of the basket so that the lid can be pressed down into it.

As with handles, some aesthetic judgment and experience will be helpful in deciding what kind of lid to use and how to construct it.

A twisted handle. A foundation rod was used, over which a grouping of smaller reeds was twisted.

A wrapped handle. The simplicity of this handle is compatible with the style of its melon basket.

Decoration Techniques

Basketry is often decorated with designs or colors woven into the structure, with materials applied to the surface, or with combinations of both. This chapter describes the techniques used in decorating woven and coiled baskets.

This 10½" high Hopi Indian coiled basket demonstrates their Palulukon design. Note the animal figures, the limited but effective use of beading in the center of the basket, the small handle, and the graduated finish. Photo by Carmelo Guadagno. Courtesy of the Museum of the American Indian, Heye Foundation. From the William Randolph Hearst Collection.

Decorations for Coiled Basketry

BEADING

Beading is a technique for decorating coiled baskets that has nothing to do with beads. Its name refers to the small floats or "beads" of decorative material that are laid onto the exterior of the basket.

Many natural materials may be used for beading, including corn husks, split wheat straws, and split palm leaves. Manufactured materials such as ribbons, synthetic raffia, and plastic may also be used as decorative elements to great effect.

To begin the process, lay a strip of decorative material (usually contrasting the structural elements in color or texture) on the surface of the foundation being stitched. Continue with the coiling stitch and cover this decorative material with stitches to secure. When a float of decorative material is desired, pick up this material and stitch *behind* it and over just the foundation. When the "bead" is the correct length, replace the decorative material on the foundation and secure with stitching once again. Thus, the coiling stitches will sometimes lie behind the decoration (and be concealed by it) and sometimes lie on the outside of the basket (see diagram). "Beads" may vary in length and may even be worked into intricate designs.

Beading

KLIKITAT (or imbrication)

Like beading, *klikitat* is a process of stitching decorative elements on the outer surface of coiled baskets; the decoration is never visible on the interior. However, the effect is that of a tile or shingle roof rather than that of a flat float of material. Here again, a wide variety of materials may be used, from corn husks to raffia to ribbons to yarn.

To begin the process, lay a strip of decorative material on the outside surface of the foundation and cover the end with coiling stitches to secure. (When there are consecutive rows of imbrication, the best stitch to use is the Plain stitch, because it will not obscure the decoration. Otherwise, use the Figure-Eight—it is the most stable coiling stitch and it will secure the decorative material very well.) When the shingled effect is desired, lift the decorative material and fold it back on itself (see diagram). Secure the fold in place with the coiling stitch. Repeat the process, with a stitch or two securing each fold. The folds of imbricating material conceal the stitches and a shingled effect is predominant.

If you choose braided material or round material, such as yarn, a looped surface is created, and if the imbrication is done extensively, the decorative effect will be similar to that of a knotted rug. You may also pull up large loops of flat or round decorative material before folding it back on itself.

As with beading, limited areas or the entire basket surface may be imbricated. Take care when stitching each successive row not to damage the decoration of the previous row.

Although there are more decorative techniques within this category, beading and klikitat offer a wide variety of design effects.

Klikitat

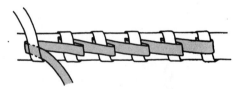

In these diagrams, the spacing between stitches has been exaggerated for clarity. In actuality, stitches should be close to each other, covering the foundation. The tone indicates the decorative material.

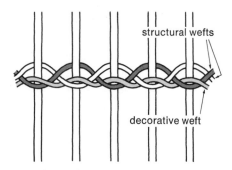

structural wefts

decorative weft

False embroidery. The decorative element does not appear on the inside of the basket.

Jacqueline Davidson's "Albatross Basket," 9" high, is twined in yarn over polished India cord and decorated with albatross feathers.

Woven Decoration for Twined Basketry

FALSE EMBROIDERY

False embroidery is a technique so called because, while giving the appearance of true embroidery, which would be applied after the basket is constructed, false embroidery is actually applied during construction and appears only on the outside of the basket.

Three pieces of material are used in addition to the warp (see diagram). Two act as the regular weft, forming a half-twist between warps, as usual. The third, or decorative, element never passes behind the warps. Rather, it wraps the length of weft lying in front of each warp, in turn, and creates decorative stitches that slant in the opposite direction to the plain twined background.

Many variations of this technique have been developed and contribute greatly to the design variety available in twined baskets. The Tee, or lattice twining, of the California Pomo Indians is an especially exciting example.

Applied Decorations

A simpler and faster method of decorating baskets is to apply various ornaments to the exterior surfaces. Traditional baskets of the American Indians reveal porcupine quills, beads, shells, feathers, leather fringes. Beads and leather are frequently found on African baskets, the leather being both decorative and functional, as it protects high-wear areas.

The contemporary basketmaker has the use of these traditional materials as well as the entire range of modern synthetics and imports available from suppliers. Short lengths of plastic tubing may be used as easily as the popular African trade beads.

SHELLS AND BEADS

Shells and beads are applied to baskets in basically the same manner. In coiled baskets they are most frequently strung onto a strong, fine thread, which is carried along the foundation until each ornament is needed. Carefully placed stitches will hold the beads or shells in place. Variations in technique that allow forming bead pendants or special edging to finish the rim of a basket are easily developed.

Shells and beads decorate twined baskets less frequently, but they can be used. The weft can become the holding cord for the ornaments, or an inconspicuous thread can be carried with the weft.

FEATHERS

As is the case with beads and shells, feathers are applied most often to the surface of coiled baskets. However, they tend to be quite fragile and must be handled with care. Originally taken from the basketmaker's natural environment, feathers are now most often purchased from sup-

Left: The miniature Peruvian-stitched basket by Rachel Seidel Gilman is made of natural raffia and decorated with feathers and glass beads. *Center:* Nancy Bess used waxed linen on jute for her covered basket and decorated the exterior with coconut shell beads. *Right:* Antique buttons were stitched in place around the rim of Susan Goldin's raffia basket.

pliers who specialize in fibers and materials for their ornamentation or from millinery suppliers (see Suppliers, page 64).

To attach feathers, lay the exposed vane of the feather against the foundation and at a 45° angle to the coil. Point the tip of the feather downward to avoid getting it caught in the stitching of the next coil. Stitch over the exposed vane one or more times as required to secure. Feathers may be overlapped to cover the entire surface.

LEATHER, YARN, RAGS, AND RIBBON

The heading of this category could be as long as the paragraph that follows. If the decorative material is flexible, it can be knotted or stitched onto almost any basket surface. Even if the material is rigid, it can be lashed in place.

Regardless of the material chosen and the method used to secure, always keep in mind the total basket. Until you become more self-confident about the actual construction techniques and more familiar with the materials used, you may want to make small samples on which you can experiment without getting involved with starts and finishes. Use varied materials in such samples to see how they modify and complement each other.

Once you start constructing actual baskets, the piece must work as a whole. You might, for example, twine a basket, concentrating on shape, and then add an ornamental rim or a row of feathers for contrast. Remember, here, that the edging must balance and not overwhelm the rest of the basket. Or you may decide to introduce a new color or material to emphasize an area you wish to draw attention to. On one side of a coiled basket, for instance, plan a small geometric pattern in a high contrast material—perhaps felt or strips of metallic foil. (If it helps, work the pattern out on graph paper first.) Try eventually to go beyond the obvious or most convenient.

Combining Fiber Techniques

Renie Breskin Adams combined macramé and stitchery in his 3½" tall, coiled rayon basket.

This detail of Susan Aaron-Taylor's "Ma Mask" reveals a unique combination of quilting and coiling. Photo by Harry William Taylor.

Although it often happens that we find baskets made entirely in one technique—coiling, plaiting, wickerwork, or twining—it is quite natural that these techniques be combined with one another and, in the growing world of contemporary fiber crafts, that they be combined with other textile arts such as weaving, crochet, and macramé, as well.

In traditional baskets, woven techniques are often combined. The cedarbark baskets of the Nootka Indians are formed with a base in checkerwork and the sides done in various twining techniques. Wickerwork baskets of willow or reed often have some rows of twining for textural contrast or for structural purposes.

Coiling, as a stitching and not a weaving technique, is another matter. With the exception of some coiled baskets that utilize plaited or twined centers, rarely are woven and coiled basketry techniques combined in traditional baskets.

The modern basketmaker, however, has broken with tradition, and it is possible to find contemporary baskets in which coiling is combined with twining, plaiting, or wickerwork. Sometimes the woven elements are worked separately and then attached to the coiled ones; sometimes they are not attached, but merely placed alongside one another to complement and contrast with one another.

Similarly, just as one may now relate coiling and twining techniques, one may combine basketry techniques with other fiber arts. The plain weave and twills of wickerwork and plaiting are precisely the same as those of onloom weaving; twining has long been a weaving technique used in the making of rugs and bags; the extension and combination of these techniques with on-loom weaving techniques is natural.

Crochet and macramé are becoming increasingly popular techniques for creating baskets; when combined with the more traditional basketry techniques, the results are both the container shapes long associated with the term *baskets* and unique sculptural forms, wall and ceiling hangings, and environments. It is similarly possible to combine basketry techniques with knitting, stitchery, or any fiber art, in order to create new textiles. The basket on page 31 shows an imaginative use of knitting, crochet, and checkerwork.

The nature of the materials available and the scale of pieces made in both traditional and combined techniques have also changed. Woven baskets have become large, soft, and fibrous, with the weight of heavy fibers previously used only for wall hangings and woven sculptures. Coiled or wrapped elements have been used to enrich the surfaces of weavings, to connect sections of woven elements, and as a method of finishing off the sometimes troublesome warp ends after a piece is taken off the loom. Again, the materials used may vary from the finest metallic threads to the heaviest manila ropes used in industry and shipping.

None of the textile arts remains separate from the rest, and the challenge and excitement of this rapidly expanding field has proved irresistible to many craftspeople.

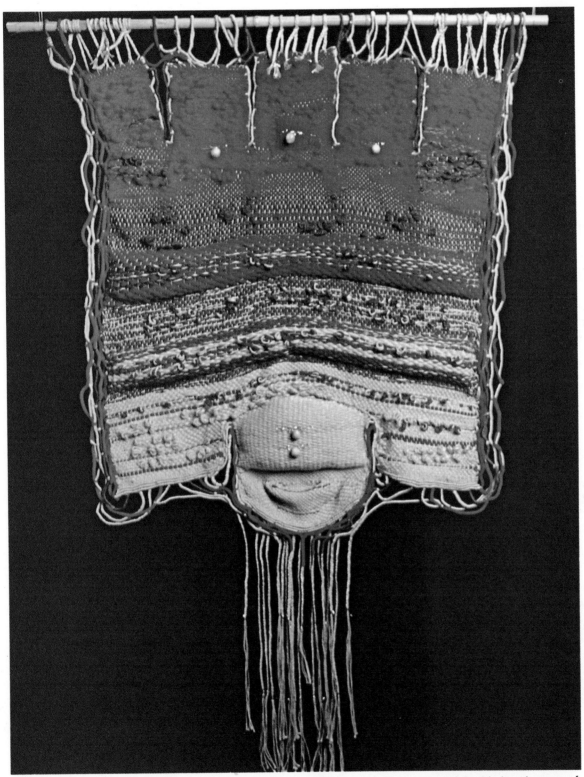

"Roots," 55″ x 39″ x 3″, a low-relief tapestry woven on a loom, has a coiled, wrapped, braided, and macramé finish. By Rachel Seidel Gilman. Ceramic beads by Sue Stephens. Photo by Clayton J. Price.

Projects

Although the following step-by-step projects were designed to include a representative cross section of methods and a wide variety of materials, they barely touch on the possibilities afforded by these fiber techniques. Each project can be readily adapted for further work and, we hope, will stimulate experimentation that will reflect each basketmaker's own sensitivity to materials, color, and design.

Note: Within each major technique category (coiling, twining, and so on), the projects progress from simple to complex. *Read all directions through completely before starting any project, and review all diagrams noted.* Sometimes a variation of the start or stitch called for is used, and the procedure for working is explained in the directions. The amount of material actually needed for one project will vary considerably from one person to the next due to differences in working tension; we have given generous estimates for each project.

Below: Coiled buttons with yarn and button backings. One of the buttons shows a central knot of a contrasting color. *Right:* This planter is light enough to be hung by fishline. The wide, flat, decorative edge was accomplished by stitching the final two coils as one.

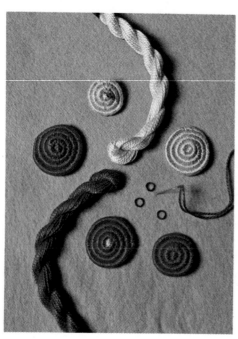

Coiled Projects

BUTTONS

Finished Size: 1½-inch diameter

Materials: 10 yards 2-ply cotton embroidery thread
embroidery needle
small metal jewelry loops or button backings
scissors

Techniques: Central Knot start for a round basket (page 19)
Plain stitch (page 21)
splicing binder (page 23)
graduated finish (page 25)
color change (optional)

Directions: Cut six 1-yard lengths of 2-ply cotton and form the Central Knot start for a round basket. When all twelve strands comprise the foundation, begin the Plain stitch, using the same material as binder. Remember to wrap *away* from you and *over* the top when using this stitch. (When using cotton embroidery thread, which has little surface fiber, extra care must be taken in placing individual stitches; each is clearly defined.) Splice new binder as needed.

To maintain complete coverage of the foundation and to ensure clearly defined coils with this particular stitch, increase the number of wraps after the first row so there will be two wraps for each stitch.

Continue working until the button measures 1½ inches in diameter— four coils around. Be sure outside coil is thoroughly covered with binding stitches, closely packed and parallel, to prevent unnecessary wear on this high-stress area. Finish by tapering the foundation bundle over the last inch until only three strands of cotton are left. Stitch this to the preceding coil, and stitch back over several coils to secure. Stitch metal loop to back of central knot.

Special Hints: For smaller, 1¼-inch buttons, use approximately 3 yards of binder for three coils. For central knot of contrasting color, use one shade for knot start only and use a second shade for binder.

PLANTER

Finished Size: 5 by 7 inches

Materials: 1 pound natural raffia—binder
12 yards sea grass—foundation
no. 18 blunt tapestry needle
scissors

Techniques: Circular start for round basket (page 15)
Peruvian stitch (page 20)
splicing binder (page 23)
graduated finish (page 25)
decorative edge (optional)

Directions: For Circular start, soak last 3 inches of sea grass until flexible. With sea grass it is easier to unply the end and taper over 1-inch length *before* wrapping tail and foundation with binder. Do so, and then thread needle with single length of raffia for binder, and proceed with Circular start for round basket. (No additional foundation material need be removed in order to complete the start.) *Note:* The binder is wrapped *toward* the basketmaker for the Peruvian stitch.

On the base, the Peruvian stitch will create a radiating pattern with its two to three wraps between long stitches. On the basket sides, the long stitches create a series of diagonal lines. As the sides slope gradually outward, the number of wraps between long stitches or the number of long stitches themselves must be carefully increased in order to maintain these diagonal lines. Further, the diagonal will be emphasized if an effort is made to keep the raffia untwisted and relatively flat and if long stitches are not pierced.

The 5-inch-diameter base is created in eight coils and an additional twenty-one coils complete the 7-inch sides. Splice binder as needed. The top edge can be finished simply by tapering the foundation over a 2-inch area and stitching back to secure end.

For a more decorative edge, as in our sample project, stitch the last two coils as if they were one. This simple technique creates a wider, flat edge that is compatible with leafy plants. Again, use a graduated finish for ending the foundation.

Special Hints: Rather than cutting off the exact length of sea grass needed for project, simply free one end of the bundle to begin with. This process allows maximum freedom of design, as size and scope of project can readily be expanded without need for splicing foundation.

Dampening raffia slightly will allow easy manipulation, but soaking is not necessary. When selecting raffia, avoid pieces already split and shredded. They can be used as a foundation bundle for another project.

Remember to line all baskets to be used as planters with foil or plastic before inserting pot.

OVAL BREAD BASKET

Finished Size: 7½ by 10 by 2 inches

Materials: approximately 1 pound natural raffia—binder
approximately 5 yards round reed (⅛-inch diameter)—foundation
no. 18 blunt tapestry needle
scissors
sandpaper (optional)

Techniques: Oval start (page 18)
Figure-Eight stitch for basic structure (page 20)
Mariposa stitch for decorative coil (page 21)
splicing reed foundation and binder (page 23)
wrapped edge with open structural handles (page 25)
graduated finish (page 25)

Directions: Soak length of round reed in warm water until flexible

enough to bend slowly back on itself. Make first bend 6 inches from end to form central row of basket. Use two strands of natural raffia for binder and form classic Oval start with Figure-Eight stitch.

Continue stitching until nine rows are coiled around the original length of reed. Then begin shaping the sides by placing the tenth coil slightly *on top of* the ninth, rather than next to it. The thirteenth coil is done in the Mariposa stitch. Follow by three coils of Figure-Eight.

The final (sixteenth) coil includes handles wrapped with the binder. Anchor with several very tight Figure-Eight stitches just before and after forming the open handles, as these are high-stress areas for the binder. Taper the foundation for a graduated finish.

Note: Because the project is designed so that the Mariposa knots will be visible on only one side of the basket—the inside—you will work with the *inside* base of the basket facing you; thus, you will be stitching on the basket side *opposite* you (that is, farthest away from you).

Special Hints: Unlike the synthetic version, natural raffia is irregular in length and width. To help compensate for this, thread two lengths end-to-end, with the narrow end of the first aligned with the wide end of the second and the ends twisted slightly on each other.

When splicing round reed for foundation, take care to do so on side of basket, rather than at points of maximum curve.

Reeds must be resoaked to make first several curves only.

Oval Bread Basket. The texture of the slightly twisted raffia is even more evident in the detail photo of the Mariposa stitches, which are visible only on the inside of the basket.

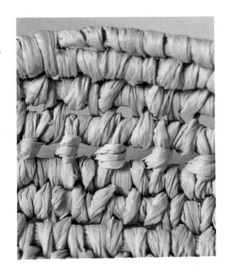

The trinket basket and its attached lid were designed to create a unified color effect.

TRINKET BASKET

Finished Size: 7 by 5½ inches

Materials: 10 yards 3-ply jute (3/16-inch diameter)—foundation
20 yards white 3-ply wool yarn—foundation and binder
25 yards burgundy 3-ply wool yarn—binder
10 yards orange 3-ply wool yarn—binder
no. 18 blunt tapestry needle
scissors

Techniques: first Square start for a round basket (page 16)
Figure-Eight stitch (page 20)
change in foundation material
color change (page 24)
fitted lid with rim
graduated finish for basket and lid (page 25)

Directions: Cut six strands of white wool 18 inches long, and proceed with the first Square start for a round basket. Use same wool for binder, and, after the first coil is complete, change to the Figure-Eight stitch, remembering to wrap *away* from you.

At this point the foundation material of bundled wool strands is changed to 3-ply jute. To do so while maintaining a constant foundation diameter, taper (unply) both the jute and the wool strands over a 2-inch length. Tie tapered areas together with thread, if necessary, for stability. Keep stitches especially firm during this transition.

Proceed, using white wool for the binder through the four coils needed to complete the base and the first three coils of the sides. Increase the number of wraps between Figure-Eight stitches, as needed, for complete coverage of the foundation.

For shaping the sides, each of the first six coils is placed on top of and slightly to the *outside* of its predecessor, the seventh coil is placed directly on top of the sixth, and each of the last five coils is placed slightly to the *inside* of its predecessor.

To change binder color, proceed as if binder were to be spliced when it ran out. Take great care to always introduce new color at the same point in the basket circumference—namely, at what will be the back where a new coil begins. In this way, color will build up uniformly and will be as horizontal to base as possible.

Continue with this modified Figure-Eight stitch (with added wraps) and note how the second color, burgundy, "bites" into the previous white coil, forming the distinctive design pattern.

The color sequence of the binder and the number of coils in each color are given in the chart at right.

Taper the basket foundation for a graduated finish.

The fitted lid is begun with the same Square start; again use six strands of white wool and again substitute jute for foundation after the first coil. Note the difference in shaping, with each of the first six coils of white placed directly on top of previous coil. Coils seven through ten are placed more to the outside of the previous coils to create the flare needed to match the circumference of the basket.

The last two coils of the lid use the burgundy yarn as binder, giving an optical effect of continuity; that is, the band of burgundy color is a continuous unit, even though part is contributed from the basket and part from the lid.

The final (eleventh) coil of the lid is placed to the inside of the previous one and forms a rim. The stitching procedure is the same, and the foundation is tapered for a graduated finish.

The lid is stitched to the basket with burgundy wool. At the back of the basket (point where all color changes took place), join the basket to the lid with long vertical stitches, stitching over the top two rows of the basket and the bottom row of the lid. Stitch from right to left, placing each stitch next to and parallel with the previous one. Cover an area of about 1½ inches, thus securing lid to basket and effectively concealing the graduated finish of both. Pass needle under several stitches to secure end of yarn, and trim.

Special Hints: When working on any fitted lid, keep the basket nearby and hold the two parts together frequently. Together they are to create a whole and must, therefore, be compatible in shape, scale, size, and color.

basket		
for base:	white	4 coils
for sides:	white	3 coils
	burgundy	3 coils
	orange	3 coils
	burgundy	3 coils

lid		
for top:	white	2 coils
for sides:	white	7 coils
	burgundy	2 coils

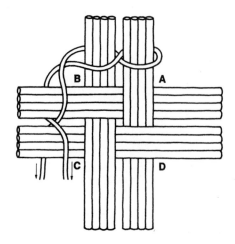

Simple woven base with twining begun

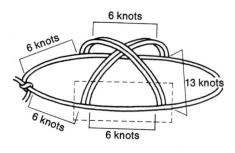

Correct spacing of warps, including handles, for twined pouch bag. (Remember that each knotted length forms two warps.) The dotted line indicates the area that is shown in the detail below.

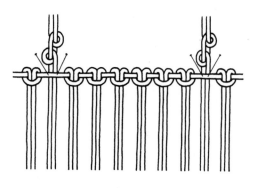

Pinning the handle warps to the holding cord

Woven Projects

TWINED WOOL BASKET

Finished Size: 4 by 5½ inches

Materials: 22 feet 5-ply jute—warp
40 feet single-ply wool ("Berber," ⅛-inch diameter)—weft
crochet hook
scissors

Techniques: simple woven start (following diagram)
Plain twining (page 36)
flared edge
abrupt finish variation (page 40)

Directions: After cutting sixteen 16-inch lengths of jute for the warp, use diagram as a guide for laying out materials for the woven base. Cut a 10-foot length of wool for weft, fold in half and slip fold down over first warp at point A. Twine around the perimeter of the woven area, placing half-twists between groups of four warps. After twining two complete rows around base, begin placing half-twists between *pairs* of warps, rather than between groups of four. The sides will come up automatically. Continue for thirteen rows of twining, holding work in hand to encourage proper shaping and tension.

Leave ¾-inch of uncovered warp between fifteenth and sixteenth rows, and then twine over single warps for final four rows to create flare at top. Trim warp to 1 inch and unply at top for fringe effect. .

Use crochet hook to pull dangling weft down under several rows of twining, and trim excess.

Special Hints: Rug wool may be used as weft with similar results.

TWINED POUCH BAG

Finished Size: 14 by 12 inches (plus handle length)

Materials: 52 yards 5-ply jute (¼-inch diameter)—warp
75 yards green rug yarn (3-ply)—weft
65 yards brick rug yarn (3-ply)—weft
10 yards peach rug yarn (3-ply)—weft
no. 18 blunt tapestry needle
scissors

Techniques: Starting at the Top for twined bag (page 34–35)
Lark's Head knot edging (page 35)
Plain twining over single warps (page 36)
two-color weft patterning (page 39)
fringe edge
splicing weft (page 39)
macramé handle

Directions: Cut a 30-inch length of jute to act as a holding cord for the top edge of bag. From the same material, cut thirty-seven warps of 40 inches each and secure around holding cord using Lark's Head knots. *Note:* Each 40-inch length becomes *two* 20-inch warps when knotted. See diagram for proper spacing of warps and handle warps.

For the handles, cut four 120-inch lengths of jute. Take two lengths for each handle and tie them together about 20 inches from the end. Drop knot over knob of drawer or door and proceed (maintaining even tension) to do reverse half-hitches (see diagram) until only 20 inches remain unknotted. Remove and repeat process for second pair of 120-inch cords. When completed, use straight pins or spring-type clothespins to attach handles in proper position on holding cord (see diagram). *Note:* The unknotted handle ends form additional warps. With this technique, the handles are in no danger of pulling away from the bag.

Remove holding cord from board and tie in a circle with an overhand knot. Cut a 6-foot length of green rug yarn, fold in center, and slip fold over the warp end directly next to large knot on holding cord. Proceed around circumference of bag with plain twining. Be sure half-twist is formed so that warps are completely wrapped in yarn. Maintain even tension on weft and push each row of weaving firmly against previous rows. Splice weft as needed.

Remember, in twining, two colors of weft can be used simultaneously to create vertical stripes. Follow the color sequence at right to create the band effect used in the sample bag.

Be sure to always change colors at the same point (where twining first began, directly below knot on holding cord), so that rows build evenly.

For fringe at bottom of bag, trim all warp ends to the same length. Final rows of twining will join front of bag to back. Lay bag on a flat work surface and smooth out so that one warp from the front lies directly on top of one warp from the back. Twine across bag, treating one warp from front and one from back (lying directly on top of each other) as if they were one. Be sure to keep them from sliding to a side-by-side position. When you reach the other side of the bag, flip the entire work over (side-to-side) and twine the final row in the same way. Trim the weft to about 2 inches and stitch into woven area of bag (see Splicing, page 39). Use tip of needle to push final rows of twining up against previous ones. Stitch any weft ends left dangling into woven area of bag.

Special Hints: Even tension on the weft is crucial in shaping twined work. Concentrate on this and proper formation of the half-twist.

TWINED STRING BAG

Finished Size: 7 by 9 inches

Materials: 83 yards of cotton "navy cord" (one cone)
           no. 18 tapestry needle
           scissors
           Sobo glue

Techniques: Starting at the Bottom for twined bag (page 35)
           Plain twining over single warps (page 36)
           crossed warps for openwork
           folding warps down on themselves (pages 40–41)
           addition of handles

Reverse half-hitch knots for handles. The space between knots is exaggerated for clarity. Knots should be pulled firmly into place, one right next to the other.

rows of twining	colors of weft
8	both wefts green
2	both wefts brick
5	1 brick, 1 peach
2	both wefts brick
3	both wefts green
7	1 green, 1 brick
3	both wefts brick
2	both wefts peach
1	both wefts green
4	both wefts brick
4	1 brick, 1 green
*3	both wefts green

Then reverse the sequence, starting with four rows of one brick and one green weft so that final three rows of green (*) are at very center of bag pattern.

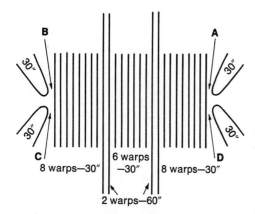

Layout of warps for twined string bag

8 warps—30" 6 warps —30" 8 warps—30"

2 warps—60"

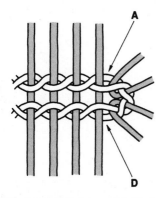

Detail showing twining at folded warp corners for first round only

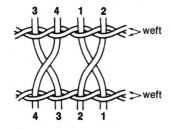

Detail of crossed warps

twining sequence

18 rows twined
crossed warps
3 rows twined
crossed warps
3 rows twined
crossed warps
18 rows twined
crossed warps
6 rows twined

Directions: After cutting twenty-six 30-inch and four 60-inch lengths of cotton cord for warp, use diagram as a guide for laying out materials on a flat work surface. Note how folded warps are incorporated next to vertical warps. The 60-inch lengths will be used for handles. Although the following is not essential, the twining process will be made easier if warp materials are laid on a large piece of paper. Then, the paper rather than the warps can be rotated clockwise, thus allowing the weaver to continue twining from right to left with a minimum amount of distortion of materials or disorientation.

Cut a 10-foot length of cord as the first weft. At the center of the warps, starting at point A, proceed twining from right to left across the width of the bag, from points A to B. The two folded warps are included in the twining between points B and C. The twining half-twist is placed between the fold of each, as shown in diagram. When both folded warps are thus twined in place, proceed across width of bag from C to D. Again, include both folded warps when twining from point D to point A. On all rows thereafter, each folded warp will be treated as two separate warps, with a half-twist made at points A, B, C, and D, as well as between the folds, as before. Two rows of twining around the base of the bag will hold warps securely in position. Material can now be hand-held to encourage proper rhythm and shaping as sides begin to develop automatically.

Splice weft as needed, but for this project, try to use longer lengths than you would normally use, as splicing is less stable with openwork and more difficult to achieve with such smooth cordage. After seventeen rows, an openwork pattern can be easily achieved by crossing warp pairs (see diagram). Thus, warps 1 and 2 cross, 3 crosses with 4, etc. Concentrate on tension, as it is more difficult to control on the twined rows just before and just after the crossed-warp areas.

Proceed with the sequence given at left.

Finish with a woven edge, folding warps down on themselves and twining three or four additional rows. Exclude from this folding process the long warps that are to be left for the handles. Each handle will be composed of four warps. To make the handles, thread each extra warp length on a needle, and stitch each parallel to corresponding warp on *opposite* side of bag. Be sure to carry warps under at least five rows of twining to secure handles. Use small amount of glue to secure them before trimming off excess length. Handles may be woven or wrapped with additional length of cord, if desired.

Special Hints: Navy cord has little, if any, surface fiber to encourage friction. As a result, cord slips on itself. The photo at right shows an alternative that might be desirable if the basketmaker is unsure of tension control in twining. About 90 yards of the material (No. 30 Mason line) were used for warp and weft. The procedure followed is essentially the same; however, the warps were cut in 50-inch lengths and the handles in 120-inch lengths. The sequence of weaving was extended beyond that used for the original project in order to balance the increased width resulting from the larger material. The handle lengths were merely knotted to join, creating a casual, but secure, finish.

Left: Twined pouch bag in rug yarn. *Right:* Two twined wool baskets. The one in the foreground shows the simple woven base. *Below:* Two twined string bags. The one at left is the project bag; the one at right was made with Mason line (see "Special Hints" on the facing page for directions).

TWINED WEED BASKET

Finished Size: 4 by 3½ inches

Materials: 7 lengths of willow cuttings—warp
1 armload honeysuckle vines—weft
1 yard cotton or linen cord
scissors or small pruning shears
awl

Techniques: preparation of natural materials (chart on page 9)
Round start—radiating spokes (page 34)
Plain twining over single warps (page 36)
plain edge—abrupt finish (page 40)
decorative handle (optional)

Directions: Trim willow growth in spring, bundle loosely, and allow to dry thoroughly. Remaining leaf buds may be rubbed off except near tips of willow saplings, but bark should be left on.

Gather honeysuckle vines in summer and tie individually in circular bundles for easy storage and soaking. Again, allow woody interior to dry completely. Handle with care to prevent breaking in storage.

Soak all materials thoroughly before beginning project. Allow at least overnight soaking for willow and one to two hours for vines. Time varies considerably with size of materials. A bathtub is ideal for willow, as entire length can be submerged without premature bending.

Trim seven willow cuttings to 24-inch lengths. Lay out in radiating-warp formation, alternating tip and base for balance. Use 3-foot length of cord to twine around center for two or three rows, and knot at back (side facing *away* from you). Cord will hold willow in position and permit maximum concentration when using vine for weft. It will be removed when basket is completed.

Twined weed basket and plaited rush mat. Note the pattern created by the 2/2 twill plaiting of the mat.

Proceed quickly with twining so that warps may be bent up for sides before they dry out. Fold one length of vine in half and slip fold down over one willow warp until it reaches woven cord area. Proceed twining around in circle for five or six rows to form base. When splicing wefts, simply leave free ends (about 2 inches) of new and old weft on inside, and proceed twining with new length.

When turning warp up for sides, handle with care and bend slowly. Resoak if necessary. Concentrate on shaping and moving along quickly. Twenty-five rows of twining formed 4-inch sides in sample project.

At top of basket, vine wefts must be resoaked, threaded down into woven area and under several rows of twining, and trimmed. An awl facilitates this process. Trim all but three or four warps that are fairly close together (try to save those with buds remaining for natural decoration) to ¼ inch to ½ inch above woven area. Wrap the remaining long warps together near their tops with a length of well-soaked vine to create the decorative "handle." Remove cord from base.

Special Hints: If work must be interrupted before project is completed, tie warps in upright position with soft yarn.

Should some warps break (and they do!), use an awl to open up space directly next to broken piece, and insert new length, leaving some side-by-side overlap for strength.

When selecting saplings and vines for this project, keep in mind that warp should be heavier than weft. The warp forms the skeletal system of the basket, and if wefts are stronger, they will dominate the warp and the basket's shape will be affected.

Size 3 round reed can be easily substituted for willow warp and size 2 round reed for vine weft.

PLAITED RUSH MAT

Finished Size: 18 by 30 inches

Materials: 1 pound natural rush (cattail leaves)
        1 dozen large, spring-type clothespins
        scissors

Techniques: preparation of natural rush (chart on page 9)
        2/2 twill plaiting (page 36)
        woven edge

Directions: Cattails should be gathered near the end of their growing season—late summer or early fall. Clip close to waterline and separate leaves. (Take care not to bend leaves when transporting them.) Dry thoroughly and turn frequently—leaves must be aired to prevent mildew. To retain as much natural color as possible, dry away from the light. When leaves are completely dry, bundle and store until needed. Rushes may also be purchased (see Suppliers list, page 64); they will already have been cured.

Sort through rush and try to select leaves that are uniform in width and strength. Soak rush in warm water until flexible, remove, and wrap in damp towel while working. Again, a bathtub is the ideal soaking place, as it allows total immersion without premature bending of material.

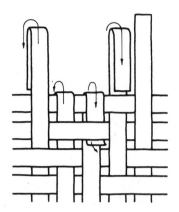

A woven edge for 2/2 twill plaiting. Note the alternating pattern—two rushes are folded back and then two are folded forward into the weaving, and so on.

On flat work area, lay out about fifteen rushes parallel to one another. Interweave at a right angle fifteen more rushes, keeping in mind that a 2/2 twill is being formed. When weaving a twill, the beginning of each vertical (or horizontal) row must be adjusted to accommodate the sequence of the weave and may seem inconsistent with the twill pattern; this adjustment is necessary to create the staggered, or stepped, effect characteristic of twills. The diagram on page 36 will show how to adjust the weaving in the beginning of each row for a 2/2 twill.

Each length must be forced tightly next to the previous one, as there will be some shrinkage in the rushes as they dry. This initial woven area of thirty rushes will stabilize material being woven in both directions.

Weave until the desired dimensions are achieved, adding rushes as needed. Trim extra rush length to about 5 inches. Remember that since this is plaiting, rows can be woven both horizontally and vertically.

Allow mat to partially dry, and take advantage of the resulting shrinkage to push material closer together. Take care to keep rushes parallel and corners of woven area squared so that a rectangle is formed, but note that natural material will yield some irregularity of shape. Use clothespins to hold weaving in place.

To finish weaving, first soak one edge of mat. When rushes are ready, turn each over on itself and reweave into the woven area of mat to secure (see diagram). To make a firm edge, it will be necessary to turn half forward (to be woven into "front" of mat) and half back (to be woven into "back" of mat). Alternate two forward and two back. This technique "traps" the final row of weaving and protects it from excess wear. After one edge is completed, finish the other edges in turn, using the same procedure described above.

Special Hints: Rushes are naturally thin at the point and fleshy at the base. Avoid using either end if possible. To break down fleshy interior without damaging outside, soak the rush, and then slowly run it over edge of table or thumbnail.

Always allow extra material. Purchase or gather at least twice as much as project requires. Remainder will be suitable for other projects.

If mat is not completed during one work session, remove rush from damp towel and allow to dry (to prevent mildew). Resoak when work resumes.

WICKERWORK SPLINT CADDY

Finished Size: 6 by 4 inches

Materials: 8 yards ½-inch splint or flat reed—warp and weft
1 bundle round reed (1/16-inch diameter)—weft
awl
sharp scissors or X-Acto blade knife

Techniques: Round start—radiating spokes (page 34)
Plain weave (page 29)
adding warp
splicing weft (page 39)
reinforced rim (page 41)

Wickerwork splint caddy

rows of plain weave	material
1	flat, narrow
11	round
1	flat, narrow
9	round
5	flat, narrow
14	round

Forming and Reinforcing Rim

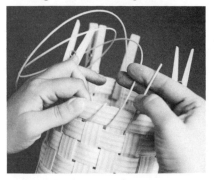

Lashing the first round

Lashing the second round in the opposite direction

Tucking reed between rim and lashing. (Above basket woven of pine strips.)

Directions: Cut eight 22-inch lengths of splint (½-inch width) and use four to create Round start. These four will form eight warps radiating from the center. In order to have the odd number necessary for wicker-work, cut one warp lengthwise to center of basket base to form two (and a total of nine).

Weave with the fine round reed in the Plain weave pattern of over-one, under-one for eight rows, remembering to treat the cut warp as two.

At this point, add the final warps (the other four 22-inch lengths cut previously) in a radiating pattern *over* the base already started. The new warps should alternate with those already woven in place (that is, lay them in the *spaces between,* not on top of, the first eight warps). Continue with plain weaving around all warps for nine rows, splicing reed as needed. Follow with three rows of weaving, using narrow, ⅛-inch splint (cut from the wider splint) to complete base of 6 inches.

Sides are formed in the sequence given at right, above.

Reinforce the top edge with rims formed of two 21-inch lengths of the ½-inch splint. Lash them on with the fine round reed in the following manner: Thoroughly soak reed before lashing. Taper end of reed and insert between rim and one warp to secure. Bring reed length out between pair of warps at front (side closest to you) of basket; carry reed over top of rim and back to inside of basket. Then bring reed out between next pair of warps. Note the angle created (see photo). Continue in this manner until one round is completed. Then change direction and lash around once again (see photo). Note the crossing formed at the top edge of the basket. Trim excess of round reed to 1½ inches and tuck into weaving, between rim and warp or rim and lashing (see photo).

Special Hints: Remember to thoroughly soak the warps before turning up sides, and the round reed before lashing edge. Light soaking will also help in weaving the first few rows of plain weave at the center of the base.

Susan Goldin's feathered disc is twined of marline and waxed linen on glazed linen and measures 22″ in diameter and 4′ in hanging length. A detail is shown on page 38. Photo by Steve Anderson.

Back Cover. *Top left:* Alice Wansor's split ash basket includes a band of cedar bark for detail on twill woven sides. *Top right:* Kari Lønning used barberry and walnut dyes for her reed melon basket. *Below:* Susan Goldin's shallow coiled basket, 8″ in diameter, is made of waxed linen binder on a jute foundation. A Plain stitch was used.

Outstanding Basketry Collections

The following museums are also a good source for basketry books, pamphlets, photographs, and slides.

American Museum of Natural History
Central Park West at 79th Street
New York, New York 10024

Denver Art Museum
100 West 14th Avenue Parkway
Denver, Colorado 80204

Lowie Museum of Anthropology
University of California
Berkeley, California 94720

Museum of the American Indian
Broadway at 155th Street
New York, New York 10032

Bibliography

General

Allen, Elsie. *Pomo Basketmaking.* Healdsburg, Calif., Naturegraph, 1972. Pomo coiled start; some wickerwork techniques.

Denver Art Museum Leaflet Series. Denver, Colo. Pamphlets on specific techniques.

Harvey, Virginia. *The Techniques of Basketry.* New York, Van Nostrand Reinhold Co., 1974. Classic and contemporary coiled and woven basketry techniques.

Harvey, Virginia, and Tidball, Harriet. "Weft Twining," *Shuttle Craft Guild,* Monograph 28. Santa Ana, Calif., HTH Publishers, 1969. Twining variations.

Meilach, Dona. *A Modern Approach to Basketry.* New York, Crown Publishers, Inc., 1974. Coiling, twining, crochet, macramé.

Navaho School of Indian Basketry. *Indian Basket Weaving.* New York, Dover Publications, 1971. Several classic coiling procedures.

Newman, Sandra. *Indian Basket Weaving.* Flagstaff, Ariz., Northland Press, 1974. Specific Indian basketry techniques.

"Plaiting" and "Twined Baskets," reprinted from *Arts and Crafts of Hawaii.* Bernice Bishop Museum, Special Publication 45. Honolulu, 1964. Plaiting and twining.

Rio Grande Press Publications. Glorieta, N. Mex. Hardbound reprints on history and techniques of Indian basketry.

Rossbach, Ed. *Baskets as Textile Art.* New York, Van Nostrand Reinhold Co., 1974. Analysis of international basketry and techniques.

Natural Basketry

Hart, Carol and Dan. *Natural Basketry.* New York, Watson-Guptill Publications, 1976.

Tod, Osma Gallinger. *Earth Basketry.* New York, Bonanza Books, 1972.

Natural Dyeing

Adrosko, Rita. *Natural Dyes and Home Dyeing.* New York, Dover Publications, 1971.

Dye Plants and Dyeing, A Handbook. Brooklyn Botanic Garden. Brooklyn, 1964.

Lesch, Alma. *Vegetable Dyeing.* New York, Watson-Guptill Publications, 1970.

Natural Plant Dyeing, A Handbook. Brooklyn Botanic Garden. Brooklyn, 1973.

Suppliers

The following is a partial list of suppliers from whom you can order by mail.

Creative Handweavers
P.O. Box 26480
Los Angeles, **Calif.** 90026
(unusual yarns, jute, cordage)

Naturalcraft
2199 Bancroft Way
Berkeley, **Calif.** 94704
(materials, cordage, beads, feathers)

Straw-Into-Gold
P.O. Box 2904
Oakland, **Calif.** 94618
(huge selection of materials plus books)

H.H. Perkins Co.
10 S. Bradley Rd.
Woodbridge, **Conn.** 06525
(flat and round reed, cane, rush)

Coulter Studios Inc.
118 E. 59th St.
New York, **N.Y.** 10022
(assorted yarns, jute, cordage)

Note: A charge for samples is not uncommon.